China's New Architecture

Christian Schittich

China's New Architecture

Returning to the Context

Birkhäuser
Basel

Contents

Christian Schittich

China's Current Architecture: On the Rediscovery of Context and the Yearning for Special Places

Along with spectacular prestige projects and skyscrapers rising ever higher into the skies above urban centers, many European observers associate contemporary building in China above all with the rapidly and uncaringly erected residential and office blocks that are shaping the current image of entire cities.

Since the then state president Deng Xiaoping introduced his fundamental economic reforms almost four decades ago, the country has been undergoing a process of urbanization unprecedented throughout the world. For a long time architectural development was unable to keep pace with the tremendous building boom that this process has produced. The need for building space has seen entire cities and old towns flattened within a few years, only to be replaced by faceless, uniform structures designed for the most part by gigantic state planning departments. These design conglomerates, which often comprise more than 1,000 employees, are still typical of contemporary China. However, over the past few years, a new generation of architects has been increasingly stepping into the spotlight. Its members have often been educated in the West before returning to their homeland in order to run private firms, something which has been permitted for only the last quarter century.

This new and adventuresome generation is notable for its individual designs and solutions. However, its representatives are above all decisively focused on combining the distinctive qualities of their country with a contemporary architectural vernacular. They reference local traditions on a range of very different levels without falling back on

Opposite: The South Yard, Sanjia, 2016, Mu Wei and Zhou Chao
Below: Cityscapes in Dalian and Shanghai

Top: History Museum, Ningbo, 2009
Above: Wall detail, Xiangshan Campus, Hangzhou, 2007, Amateur Architecture Studio

traditional forms. It is precisely this approach that often leads to particularly vibrant and expressive buildings, which are appearing ever more frequently in international publications.

In 2012 Wang Shu, one of the most important representatives of the new, independently operating architectural community, was awarded the prestigious Pritzker Prize. Even if this recognition of such an obvious maverick remains controversial among his Chinese colleagues, it shows them that an independent Chinese architecture is capable of achieving the highest of international honors. This has provided enormous impetus for the entire profession in China. And it has also drawn the attention of architectural colleagues in the West. Not only at a national but also an international level, Wang Shu, with his office Amateur Architecture Studio, is unquestionably one of the most fascinating designers working today. His idiosyncratic architecture is conspicuously inspired by the culture of his homeland and features what are sometimes monumental but always vital forms and a rough materiality, which often results from the recycled stones and tiles he likes to use. Over a million are said to have been used on the Ningbo History Museum (2009), which towers into the sky like a massive fortress, and on the Xiangshan Campus of the China Academy of Art in nearby Hangzhou. This diversely designed complex comprising a total of twenty-one individual buildings, hardly any two of which resemble one another, was inspired by Chinese landscape painting from the eleventh century. Here, the architect was far less interested in creating a finished image than in generating a setting which can be filled with life and which changes with the seasons and over the course of time.

Architects from MAD also drew on classical landscape images and depictions of mountains in ancient ink drawings when designing Chaoyang Park Plaza in Beijing, a structure made up of a "mountain" formed by two connected office towers and several smaller residential and commercial "hills." Although conspicuously modern with its dark glazing, this reference is immediately evident in the building's organic form. Inspired by nature, this shape, according to the architects, was designed to extend the adjacent park into the city.

Ma Yansong, the founder of MAD, proudly identifies himself as China's first architect to win a significant international competition, which he did in 2006 with the Absolute World towers in Mississauga, Canada. Before establishing his own practice in 2004, Ma worked for several years with Zaha Hadid, whose formal vocabulary and design methods he is now endeavoring to adapt to the particularities of his homeland. Even though in the case of Chaoyang Park Plaza he has drawn on similar motifs to those inspiring Wang Shu, the types of architecture produced by MAD and Amateur Architecture Studio could hardly be more different, and the two studios can be seen as representing what are probably the two most extreme positions in the current generation of Chinese architects.

Above: Bridge School, Pinghe, 2009, Li Xiaodong
Below: Chaoyang Park Plaza (left: office towers, right: view of the residential complex), Beijing 2017, MAD Architects

Projects with Added Social Value

Not only their divergent architectural idioms but also the size of some of the buildings designed by Wang Shu and MAD can be described as extreme. By contrast, almost all the examples presented in the project section of this book (apart from the conversion in Shanghai) are on a significantly smaller scale. Some are located in the countryside, and quite a few of them exhibit a focus on added social value. Three of them are the result of rebuilding measures in the wake of natural catastrophes, while others are designed to improve the infrastructure in poor rural areas. Such buildings are repeatedly built in China on the initiative of and due to the high level of personal engagement of their architects. This is also true of the internationally renowned Bridge School located in a remote Hakka village in Fujian, whose designer, Li Xiaodong, himself took responsibility for finding financial backers for the project. With a small yet visually striking bridge, the

architect not only created the space required by the school but also linked two *tulou* previously separated by a creek. These two traditional residential complexes are now connected by a central, social space and thus a new communal meeting point.

Bridge renovation, Shimen, 2017, DnA_Design and Architecture

Following the unprecedented wave of urbanization referred to above, which swept hundreds of millions of former villagers into hastily erected cities – with all their attendant problems – there is now an increasing focus on the countryside in China. Many interventions are consciously aimed at revitalizing rural space and improving the quality of life there in order to counter the exodus from the land.

Another example in this context, one that is as unusual as it is impressive, can be found in the county of Songyang in Zhejiang, where the local administration has launched a variety of projects designed to stimulate the economy, promote social cohesion, and strengthen cultural identity by upgrading existing building stock. However, what is really special here is the fact that authorities have focused exclusively on well-designed and contemporary architecture. For example, over the last four years Xu Tiantian, with her Beijing office DnA, has designed more than twenty projects for Songyang and realized them with the help of local architects. All her projects have been built with the collaboration of the respective village communities and local tradespeople. They include the Brown Sugar Factory in Xing, which has improved processing conditions for local sugarcane farming and consequently increased income while also providing a community building which has a range of social functions (p. 97). Other projects include the renovation and upgrading of the bridge in Shimen, which has been given a clearly structured wooden roof that recalls local traditions and has become a social meeting point, and the restoration of old rammed earth houses in the small mountain village of Pingtian. The last two examples are indicative of a quite new tendency in China: the rediscovery of existing building stock.

Above: Village renovation, Pingtian, 2015, DnA_Design and Architecture
Below: Skywells Hotel, Wuyuan, 2017, anySCALE

The Rediscovery of Existing Building Stock

Until a few years ago the old peasant houses made of rammed earth or air-dried bricks found throughout China had little chance of survival. Everywhere they were being ruthlessly torn down and replaced by faceless new buildings made of reinforced concrete because the latter promised greater comfort than traditional structures requiring intensive maintenance. Now it is often local administrations that are providing the impetus and sometimes also financial incentives for the restoration of older buildings, often with the promotion of soft tourism in mind. Once villagers realize that visitors are prepared to travel significant distances to admire their old buildings, they begin to place greater store in their own culture. Above all people from the rapidly growing middle class living amid the noise and poor-quality air of China's major cities are increasingly seeking a break from city life in the hinterland. One result of this has been the addition of guest rooms when refurbishing peasant houses, in order to provide villagers with a source of income other than agriculture and handicraft products. Since a change in the law a few years ago that allows the commercial use of private houses, such homestays have been shooting up everywhere.

At the same time an increasing number of traditional buildings are being converted into comfortable design hotels, one example being the Skywells Hotel in Wuyuan. In this case a couple who had formerly worked in the Shanghai financial world bought an old wooden mansion and, with a great deal of their own energy, local craftsmen, and the architects from anySCALE in Beijing, restored it and converted it into a guest house.

It is not only in the countryside but also in the cities that existing building stock is being increasingly prized. This is evident not least in the case of the classical hutongs in Beijing. As late as the 1990s, these alleys formed by lines of traditional courtyard residences, like many other old city structures in China, were being demolished, only to be partly rebuilt in an altered form for the Olympic Games in 2008. However, the original stock of hutongs was so large that they survived in various areas and are now being filled with new life.

In order to illustrate the potential offered by this form of building and to ensure the survival of the old houses without converting them only into souvenir shops and restaurants, the architect Zhang Ke with his firm ZAO/standardarchitecture has been initiating a series of hutong projects. One example is his so-called Micro-Hutong conversion involving the integration into a particularly narrow courtyard of a sculptural cement structure comprising spaces that can serve as a hostel for students or as temporary living and working space for an artist. In the Micro Yuan'er project he created a meeting point for children in the area by installing a small library and a space for creative activities (p. 67), and his Co-living Courtyard project aimed to convert an existing courtyard residence into a communal living complex by combining communal spaces with tiny apartments. However, no client for the project could be found and the restored courtyard residence now houses a private school.

Above: Traditional hutong in Beijing
Below: Micro-Hutong, Beijing, 2013, ZAO/standardarchitecture

Another important architectural focus in many Chinese cities is the conversion of obsolete and disused industrial facilities. Such projects

in Shanghai are in many places focusing on art and culture as new locational factors. The West Bund Cultural Corridor project initiated by the city, for instance, envisages the revitalization of a 7-square-kilometer former harbor and industrial area with a particular focus on cultural facilities.

Above: Shanghai Power Station of Art, 2012, Original Design Studio

In this context, Zhang Ming and Zhang Zi from Original Design Studio at Tongji University converted a former power station dating from 1985 into the Shanghai Power Station of Art (2012) – China's first state museum for contemporary art – which features 10,000 square meters of exhibition area. The architects made a feature not only out of the enormous old building with its industrial relics but also the fantastic view it offers of the nearby river. At least equally as impressive – both in terms of their dimensions and their location – are the new exhibition spaces installed by Atelier Deshaus in the huge 80,000-ton silo warehouse on Minsheng Wharf (p. 123).

Apart from financing such cultural centers itself, the state is also endeavoring to encourage private investors to build museums by offering tax incentives and low-priced leases on land. One very positive addition to contemporary Chinese architecture built as a result of such incentives – and also designed by Atelier Deshaus – is the much lauded Long Museum located on the former site of a coal hopper. Along with its skillful integration of the remnants of the old industrial facility, the museum is notable for its intriguingly designed exhibition spaces, precise details, and what is for China extraordinarily high-quality workmanship.

Modern Architecture as Attraction

The well-known library on the beach in Beidaihe by Vector Architects (p. 43) has also long been one of China's contemporary architectural icons. It, too, was commissioned and financed by a private investor in order to enhance the status of the holiday resort he had built nearby. The precisely implemented Seashore Library with its markedly modern appearance has now become so popular via social media that on some days it draws more than 3,000 people. The visitors, some of whom have traveled a long way, do not come primarily to browse through books or to attend an event, but simply because they want to have been at such a popular location. Well-designed contemporary architecture in China is increasingly becoming a magnet for the public and is fulfilling an increasing yearning for special places. Some project developers have recognized this and endeavor to use targeted interventions to enhance the status of existing and newly built large-scale projects. When developers also take quality into account in this context and are prepared to pay for it, and when they above all give architects and building firms sufficient time for design and construction – and this can certainly not be taken for granted in China – the results can be extraordinary. It was such an approach that produced the Suzhou Chapel by Neri&Hu (p. 37).

Another example illustrating people's desire for a special type of architecture is the Zhongshu Bookstore in Suzhou designed in the colors of the rainbow by Wutopia Lab, which attracts so many people to a multistory shopping center that its owners do not have to pay rent. The operator's difficult business model in an age of digital media thus benefits from a concept that continues to attract entire families on their Sunday outings, even though they are often more interested in taking selfies in front of the bookshelves than the books themselves.

Long Museum West Bund, Shanghai, 2014, Atelier Deshaus

Seashore Library, Beidaihe, 2015, Vector Architects

Sensually Rough Materials and Weathered Surfaces

The high quality of construction characterizing buildings such as the Long Museum and the Seashore Library is particularly worthy of mention because it can certainly not be taken for granted in the Chinese context. On the contrary, many buildings continue to suffer from extremely slipshod construction due to what are often enormous time pressures and a glaring lack of suitably qualified specialists. It remains the case that the majority of those working on building sites are untrained former agricultural workers, none of whom, including the foreman, are capable of reading a plan. The spectrum of skilled crafts is also far smaller than in the West, and the capacity of the architect to decide on how the final construction is carried out is often based on the discretion of the building client. As a result there is often a great deal of simpler and cheaper construction than originally envisioned by the designer.

The results are new buildings which often end up looking rather unsightly after a short time and sometimes already have to be renovated after only a few years. The lack of construction quality is compounded by detail work that produces elegant and photogenic projects which quickly become dilapidated. As a result, visitors may look forward to viewing a highly publicized building only to find a rather shabby structure bereft of the vibrancy promised by the vivid images available on the Internet.

Nevertheless, it is worth pointing out that the notion of how a building should age is often completely different in China than in the West. What we already see as building damage may be regarded as inconsequential by the Chinese architect or developer. This is not least due to the fact that, like in Japan, transience is traditionally part of

Zhongshu Bookstore, Suzhou, 2017, Wutopia Lab

the building concept and sometimes even shapes a building's aesthetic. And indeed, white plaster facades of historical houses take on character only once darker patches start to appear and originally smooth gray tiles gain expressiveness through rapid weathering processes. Some architects consciously plan such effects, such as Zhang Ke, who takes pleasure in seeing the originally pristine masonry on his office gradually gain a coarse surface (p. 63). Or they deal with the inevitable marks of weathering from the outset by using rough walls that allow for constructional inaccuracies in keeping with the weathered building materials. At least from an aesthetic point of view, the fact that the lacquered steel window panels on Wang Shu's academy buildings in Hangzhou are already exhibiting large traces of rust does not create a disturbing impression. Indeed, it is due to these markings that the facades properly harmonize with the adjacent masonry made up of recycled stones.

Irrespective of such considerations, the impact of many of the best projects in China is based on their sensually rough materiality: coarse undressed stone, recycled tiles, rusting weather-resistant steel and roughly formed concrete.

Especially when it comes to designs for the countryside, many architects endeavor to create connections with local construction methods in order to anchor their buildings in the region. This repeatedly leads to buildings that exert their particular fascination through the interplay of traditional building materials and a modern canon of forms, as impressively illustrated by the Jianamani Visitor Center in Yushu (p. 91).

Like the visitor center in Yushu, all the buildings presented in the following project section are notable for the way they refer to their respective context. This can take the form of a sensitive approach to the existing building stock, parallels with local traditions, or the utilization of traditional materials. Many of the examples are characterized by a high degree of creativity and entail refreshingly unconventional solutions which make it fun to engage with them.

Although these projects present a wide range of tasks, ideas, and approaches, they need to be seen – within the enormity of China – more as the exception than the rule. At the same time, they offer grounds for hope and illustrate the exciting dynamism of current developments in the Chinese architectural scene.

Above: Architecture office, Beijing, 2015, ZAO/standard-architecture
Below: Jianamani Visitor Center, Yushu, 2013, TeamMinus

Christian Schittich

Architecture as Alive as Life Itself: In Conversation with Wang Shu

Since being awarded the Pritzker Prize in 2012, Wang Shu, who runs the firm Amateur Architecture Studio with his wife, Lu Wenyu, has numbered among China's most well-known architects. With his highly original, powerful architecture he connects with the traditions of his homeland and endeavors to harmonize inherited values and local building traditions with a contemporary design that is marked by sculptural forms and sensually rough surfaces. His buildings imbue millions of old bricks and tiles with new life.

Opposite: Cultural Complex, Fuyang, 2018, Amateur Architecture Studio
Below: Xiangshan Campus, Hangzhou, 2007, Amateur Architecture Studio

Wang Shu, why is tradition so important to you?
Over the last two or three decades we have destroyed more than 90 percent of China's traditional building stock in the cities and in the countryside. However, it needs to be considered that the disappearance of these buildings brings about changes to the way people live. Many architects hardly think about the social consequences of this gigantic building boom. But I try to learn from tradition and to create a bridge between the past and the present through the integration of traditional building methods.

What role does the use of recycled roof tiles and bricks, for which you are so well known, play in this context?
About a year before the planned completion of the Xiangshan Campus in Hangzhou, the supply of building materials began to run out. The construction manager came to me and asked if it would be possible to build not only with new but also used materials. My response was enthusiastically affirmative. In China used materials have always been utilized. They are too valuable to be simply thrown away when a building

History Museum, Ningbo, 2008, Amateur Architecture Studio

is torn down, and it used to be normal to find the walls and roofs of new buildings in some cases made out of bricks and tiles that were centuries old. These have a somewhat different shape, color, and surface to new tiles and integrate the building far better into its surroundings. They give walls a particular character and result in their aging better.

In the case of the History Museum in Ningbo, we deliberately used old stones for a part of the wall in order to create a reference to the villages that once stood at this location. Thirty beautiful traditional villages were flattened here to make way for the new business district alone. The destroyed houses now live on in the walls of the museum. And this is how the former residents of the buildings see it, too. Some of them come here again and again to look at the walls in order to remind themselves of their old homes.

When I look at your walls made of recycled building materials, I also see patterns formed by colors. In Ningbo, for example, the gray-brown of the walls is interspersed with areas of red tile. How precisely do you plan such structures?
I am not a fan of consciously designed patterns or images and I would tear anything like that down again. Rather than something decorative I look for the spontaneous, the improvised. To achieve this I rely on the creativity of my tradesmen and their ability to create stable structures out of different demolition materials. Much of the end result only emerges during building.

You run your office together with your wife, Lu Wenyu. How exactly does your collaboration function?
We have developed a particular form of collaboration. Normally I do the initial sketches and then we discuss them together. My wife is a very tough critic. Normally Lu Wenyu doesn't produce drawings herself but she has a very good feel for design and, later, the process from design to realization. In this context her involvement is decisive.

Cultural Complex, Fuyang, 2018
Wall detail and north facade,
Amateur Architecture Studio

How does the design process proceed in detail?
I start in each case with a very precise pencil drawing rendered by hand. I don't use a computer. I also don't write emails. Members of my staff then translate my hand drawing into digital form. They are themselves good freehand drawers and can read the sketches correctly. During the transfer of the drawing to the computer, we discuss the individual aspects of the design again.

How has your life changed since winning the Pritzker Prize?
Our office and I are now known to a wide public in China. Prior to the prize, people who knew about us were insiders, that is, other architects. In addition the prize has given me a certain professional weight, which is of course an advantage when it comes to negotiations with government clients.

You also brought this weight to bear in the case of your two latest projects in Fuyang and Wencun.
Yes, when the regional authorities in Fuyang asked me to design a new cultural center, I only agreed on the condition that I could also renovate a traditional village in the surroundings. After a long search we decided on the remote village of Wencun, which is around 50 kilometers west of Fuyang. Normally the state authorities in China do not have much interest in renovating villages. They would rather build museums. But for me it's very important to design or preserve something that touches the lives of normal people.

Cultural Complex, Fuyang, 2018
Interior spaces of the art gallery with bamboo-marked concrete walls (left) and curved concrete roofs (right)

What's the precise nature of the project in Fuyang and what is the basic idea behind your design?
The new cultural complex in Fuyang houses an art gallery, a history museum, and a huge archive as well as administration offices. The area around the Fuchun River has long been renowned for its beauty, and the location is the setting of a famous Chinese painting dating from the Yuan dynasty (1279–1368), which almost everyone in the country is familiar with. In traditional Chinese architecture the relationship between building and landscape was very important. This is also expressed in an idealized form in classical ink painting. For me this relationship, which has largely been lost today, is also very important, particularly here in this place. With the large curved roofs of the cultural center I tried to incorporate the surrounding mountains and in this way to enter into a dialogue with the center's environs. For the external walls and roofs we have again mainly used recycled materials in order to interlink the huge structure with its surroundings as well as with the history of the location.

And what was the objective of your village renewal project in Wencun?
Economic growth in China and the exodus from the land that is connected with it, as well as the enormous construction boom, have resulted in a rapid decrease in the number of villages in the country. Between 2000 and 2010 alone, this number fell from 3.7 million to 2.6 million. And when we lose our villages we also lose a large part of our culture and the traditional way of life, which is far more oriented to the community and nature than life in the city is. Our objective is to make life in the countryside attractive again, and the renovation of the village of Wencun is intended as an example of how this can be achieved.

And what have you done there specifically?
We have rebuilt thirty houses in Wencun and renovated a number of existing buildings. Some of these are ugly buildings, which we have now above all better integrated into the townscape.

We have developed different types of houses for our new buildings, which are all – following the traditional model – arranged around a courtyard. Apart from living areas, every house contains space for farming equipment or craft activities because it is important that people on the land are also able to make a living. We have built predominantly with natural materials as was traditionally done in the villages: natural stone and clay, bamboo and wood.

Why have you used so many different materials and different shapes in Wencun? Normally traditional villages are very uniform.
If you look around old villages, you will be surprised by the variety to be found there. And it is this variety that I am referring to. I am not interested in building in one style or restoring former appearances. And I certainly would not want to copy tradition. My aim is to use traditional materials and construction methods to make something new. But I also want each house to look a little different so that its inhabitants can more closely identify with it.

Nevertheless, it is noticeable that some parts of your houses involve a combination of numerous materials and details while others exhibit simpler forms.
That has to do with my attitude to life. Good architecture is not just about style, material, and form. Good architecture should be as alive as life itself. In this respect, details also have different functions. Some only have to serve a certain purpose such as draining off water.

Cultural Complex, Fuyang, 2018
The western facade of the adminstrative wing, which is more than 100 meters long, is animated by a mix of rough and smooth natural stone surfaces and recycled bricks and tiles on the walls and roofs.

Others, by contrast, are designed above all to make the building more alive.

How did you include the residents in the planning process?
That was quite complicated. The houses were allocated to people in a kind of lottery because there were many more applicants than there were houses. Once it was clear who would move into which houses, the new residents could propose small changes such as a larger kitchen or two central living areas instead of one as originally planned, so that, for example, the room for ancestor worship could be separated from the one containing the television.

Village renewal, Wencun, 2016
The facades of the new buildings exhibit a lively mix of materials: natural stone, rammed earth and plaster. The walls facing on-to the courtyards are made of wood and glass.

Did people have reservations about particular materials, such as rammed earth, which is now seen as antiquated in many rural areas?
When I was considering building several houses out of rammed earth, I wasn't sure at first whether this method would be accepted by the residents. The representatives of the authorities were also concerned about clay houses. However, the sequence in which the winners of the lottery were selected was also the basis of allocation – the first to be drawn was given the first choice of house. To our great surprise he chose one made of clay.

The impact of your buildings is generally based to a large extent on your use of natural materials such as stone, clay, and bamboo.

However, you coated the wood on the houses in Wencun with clear varnish, which in the case of other projects – for example, the Academy of Art in Hangzhou – soon flaked off, thereby making the facades look shabby. Wouldn't the effect be more powerful if the wooden building elements were left untreated?
Today, building with wood is very difficult in China because most people don't like it. In old houses the wood is untreated, but no one wants to live there anymore. To be in line with most people's ideas of modern life, wood needs to have a paint finish. I would only be able to insist on natural wood in a residential building if I could choose my client myself.

That's strange: People are willing to live in a house built of rammed earth but will not accept natural wood.
Yes, apparently building with clay has a better image.

The interview with Wang Shu was conducted by Christian Schittich in February 2017 in Copenhagen on the occasion of the opening of the exhibition *Wang Shu: Amateur Architecture Studio* in the Louisiana Museum of Modern Art. In December 2017 it was published in revised form in the journal *archithese* (Zurich).

Projects

11 Yushu/Qinghai

Tianquan/Sichuan

A Visitor Center with a Local Reference

Kindergarten in the Mountains

Village Reconstruction Following an Earthquake

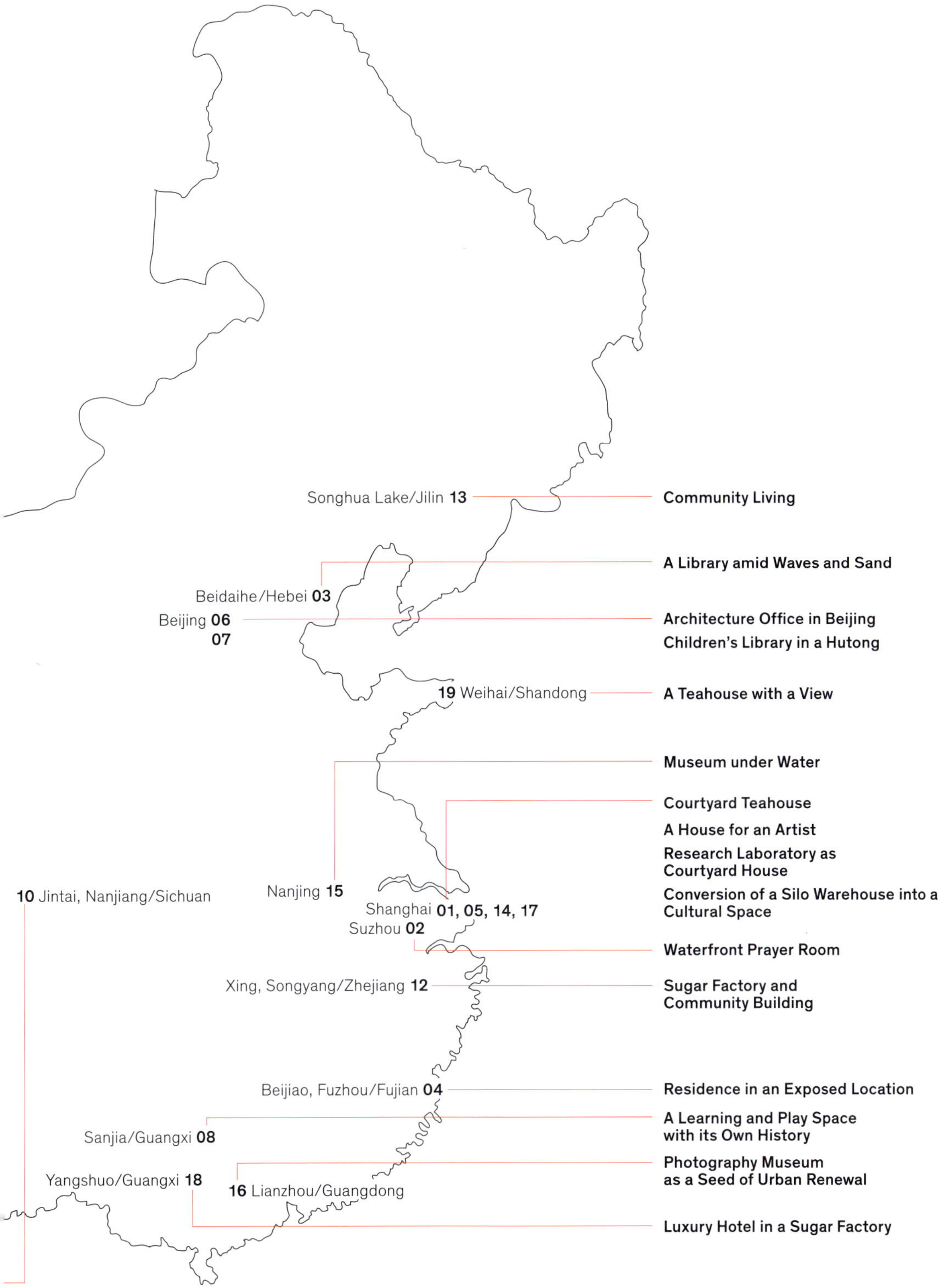
Songhua Lake/Jilin 13
Community Living
A Library amid Waves and Sand
Beidaihe/Hebei 03
Beijing 06
07
Architecture Office in Beijing
Children's Library in a Hutong
19 Weihai/Shandong
A Teahouse with a View
Museum under Water
Courtyard Teahouse
A House for an Artist
Research Laboratory as Courtyard House
Conversion of a Silo Warehouse into a Cultural Space
10 Jintai, Nanjiang/Sichuan
Nanjing 15
Shanghai 01, 05, 14, 17
Suzhou 02
Waterfront Prayer Room
Xing, Songyang/Zhejiang 12
Sugar Factory and Community Building
Beijiao, Fuzhou/Fujian 04
Residence in an Exposed Location
A Learning and Play Space with its Own History
Sanjia/Guangxi 08
Photography Museum as a Seed of Urban Renewal
Yangshuo/Guangxi 18
16 Lianzhou/Guangdong
Luxury Hotel in a Sugar Factory

01 **Atelier Deshaus** **Shanghai**

Courtyard Teahouse

The small teahouse is a good example of how a previously neglected site can be enhanced and imbued with a particular atmosphere by simple means. At the same time, Atelier Deshaus has found a way to fuse modern materials and construction with Chinese traditions without imitating historical forms. The challenge was to create a garden out of a previously neglected access area between two small office buildings used by a fashion firm in the immediate neighborhood of the architect's studio on Shanghai's West Bund. Atelier Deshaus was commissioned to design a teahouse that could provide a space for retreat from the urban environment while also catering to guests in search of sustenance. The architects positioned the new building on the very edge of a courtyard measuring around 110 square meters and shaded by the crown of an old paulownia tree, creating a continuous green area in front of the entrance. To the rear, where the L-shaped structure creates an enclosed exterior space, they have integrated the striking tree trunk in the overall composition. In the interior the black-painted steel structure contrasts with the warm wooden tones of the floor and fixtures.

Project name
Teahouse in Li Garden

Client
Private

Completion
2016

Floor area
19 m^2

Construction
Steel, glass, wood

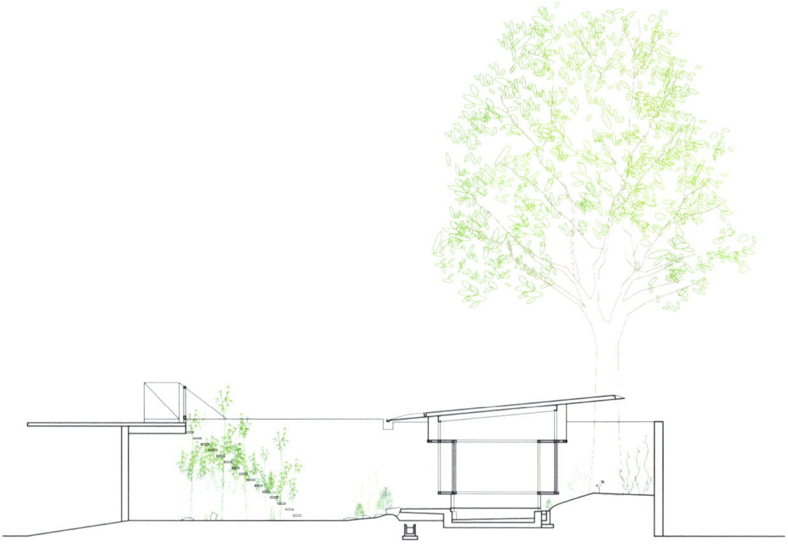

Cross section (1:200)

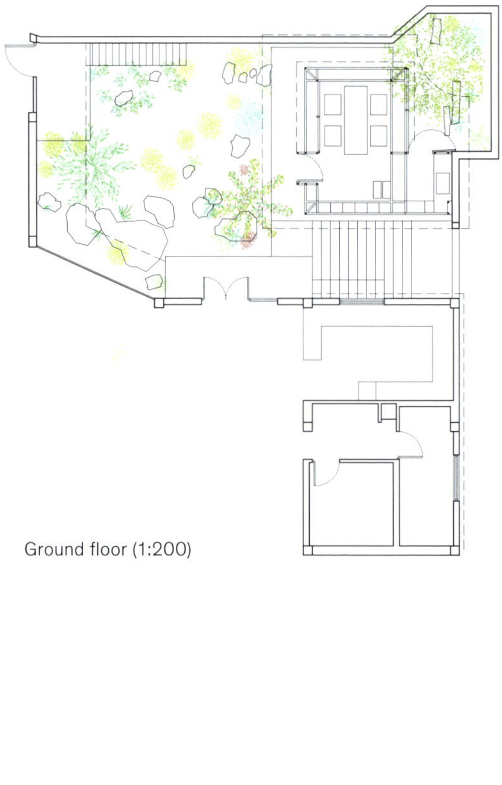

Ground floor (1:200)

The small teahouse in a courtyard between two office buildings combines Chinese tradition with modern forms and materials.

Waterfront Prayer Room

Expensive wellness hotels with attached villa resorts are on the rise in China. One of these complexes includes a chapel on the shore of a lake, which provides a contemplative prayer room for guests irrespective of their religion. On the outside the structure appears as a white cube on a base of rough brick masonry. The design language employed by the architects thus takes up motifs and colors drawn from the surroundings, such as the white plastered walls and gray tile roofs typical of Suzhou, but positions them in a new context. The white cube is composed of two layers. The inner layer is a simple box punctuated by scattered windows, while the outer layer is a perforated metal skin, a veil that alternately hides and reveals. A carefully designed pathway comprising stairs and ramps leads visitors to the 12-meter-tall prayer room. On the ground floor the space is enclosed by a rough brick wall, on the upper level by a shell of wooden slats. A laterally positioned stairway leads to the roof terrace, which offers a spectacular view over the lake. The route to the top already offers a range of framed views of the surroundings and the chapel space through the apertures in the walls. Even if not completely unambiguous in functional terms, the building is notable for its consistent design, its coordinated building materials, spatial diversity, and clear details, aspects that fulfill the growing need in China for special places.

Project name
Suzhou Chapel

Client
SANGHA Retreats

Completion
2016

Floor area
700 m²

Construction
Recycled tiles, reinforced concrete, perforated metal

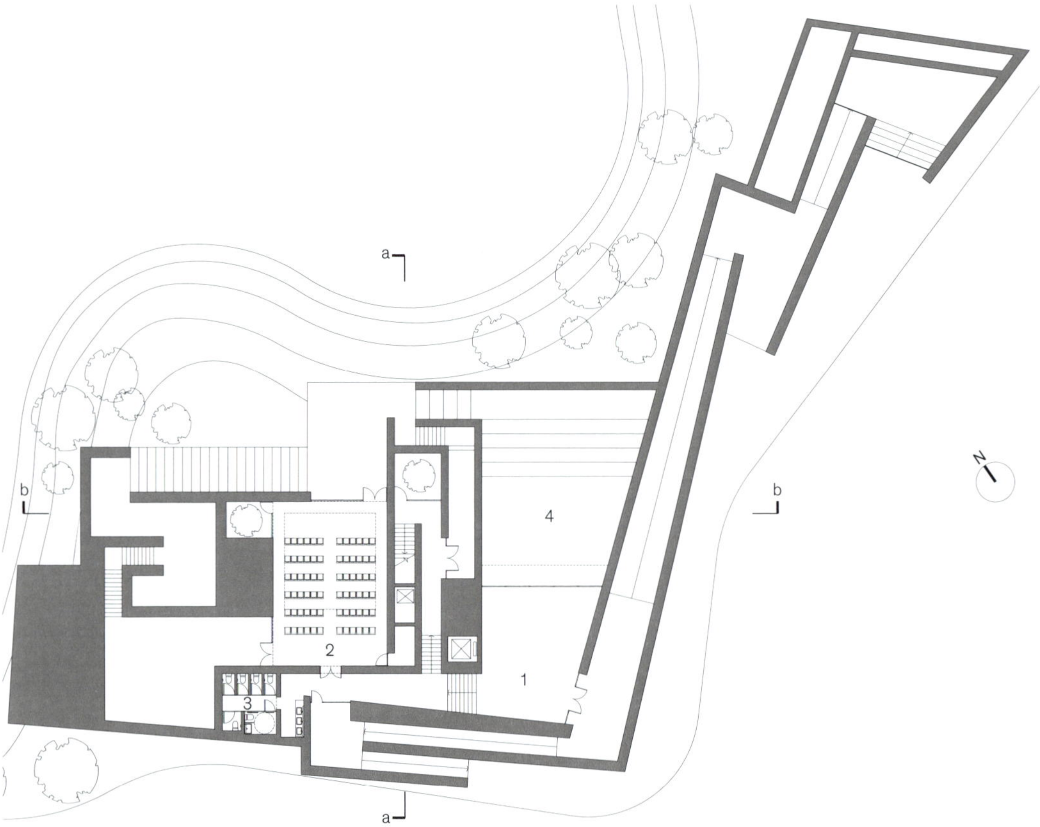

Ground floor

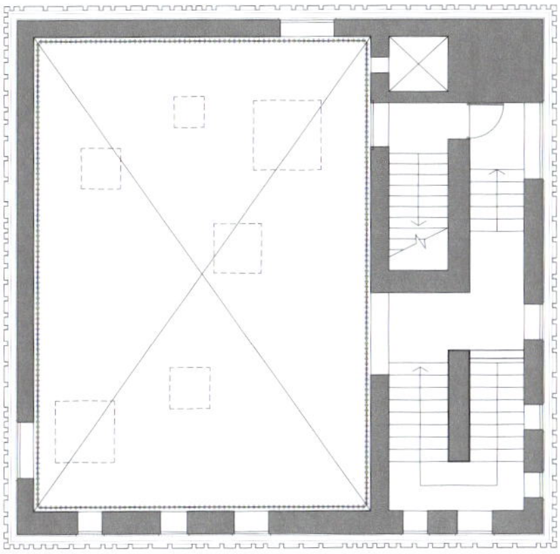

Fourth floor

Ground floor
Scale ca. 1:500

Floor plan upper levels 1–3
Scale ca. 1:250

1 Foyer
2 Main hall
3 Toilet
4 Courtyard

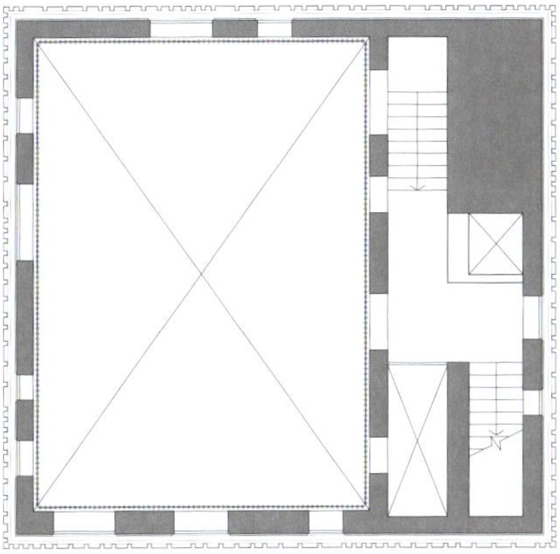

Third floor

A hard shell made of shiny white metal conceals an interior space clad with wood. The substructure is made of rough brick masonry.

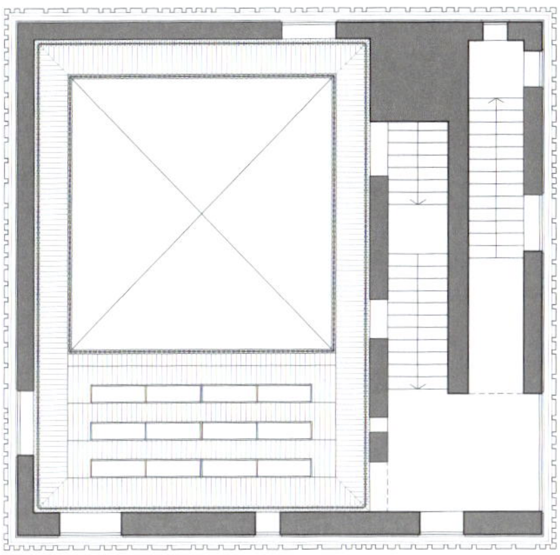

Second floor

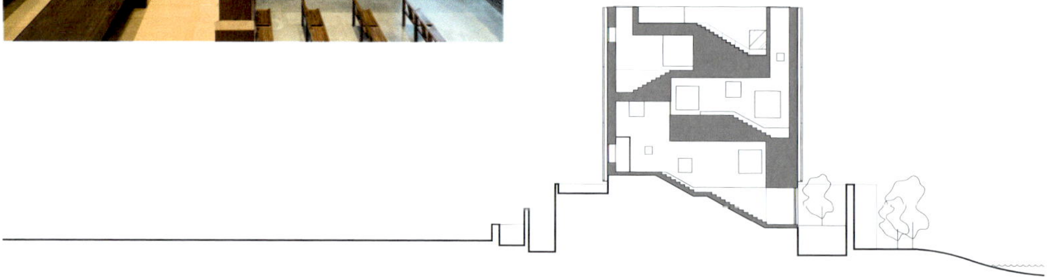

Cross section a

The abstractly designed pathway leading to the top of the structure offers diverse spatial impressions and a series of framed views into the prayer room.

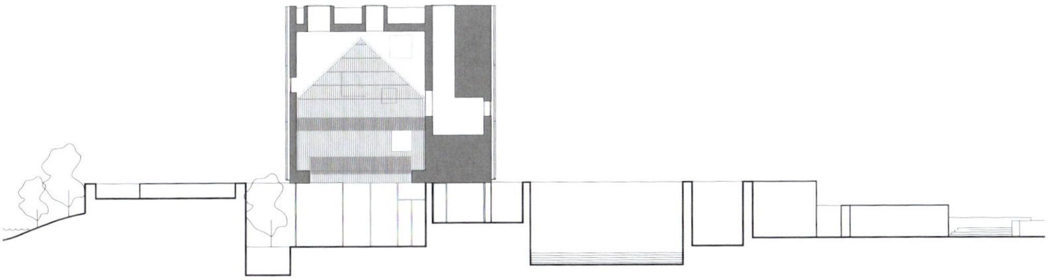

Cross section b

03 Gong Dong, Vector Architects — Beidaihe, Hebei

A Library amid Waves and Sand

A library on a beach with the sea at its doors – it sounds like a dream. A spectacular view from the reading room over the ocean with its constantly changing colors and moods, a silent sphere of meditation, sensually rough surfaces on which the rays of the sun create an interplay of light and shadow: Gong Dong, the founder of Vector Architects, devised a fascinating way to realize the vision of a developer who wanted a multifunctional cultural space for his new holiday resort. Holiday guests and residents of the district of Beidaihe, which has a population of some 70,000 and is located about three hours' drive east of Beijing, are able to browse through books here, meet with friends, or attend a theater performance. The space is basically organized into three differently designed areas. The largest of these is the bright, light-flooded reading area, which is equipped with seating platforms set higher toward the back of the space and opens onto the sea by way of a giant panoramic window. Adjacent to this area is the considerably more peaceful meditation room and a performance and event area, which is separated from the rest of the space for acoustic reasons by a small outdoor platform. The library, to which new holiday houses are now drawing rather close on the resort side of the structure, has long been far more than a place for reading or attending concerts. Fashion labels use it for photo shoots, and it is a popular meeting point for young people keen on taking selfies. With as many as 3,000 visitors a day, it is now common to wait in a queue for a while before being able to enter if you have not booked a time slot beforehand online.

Project name
Seashore Library

Client
Beijing Rocfly Investment Group

Completion
2015

Floor area
450 m²

Construction
Reinforced concrete, glass blocks, masonry

Floor plans
Scale 1:250

1 Reception
2 Book display
3 Reading room
4 Rest area
5 Bar
6 Storage
7 Office
8 Terrace
9 Meditation room
10 Activity room
11 Balcony

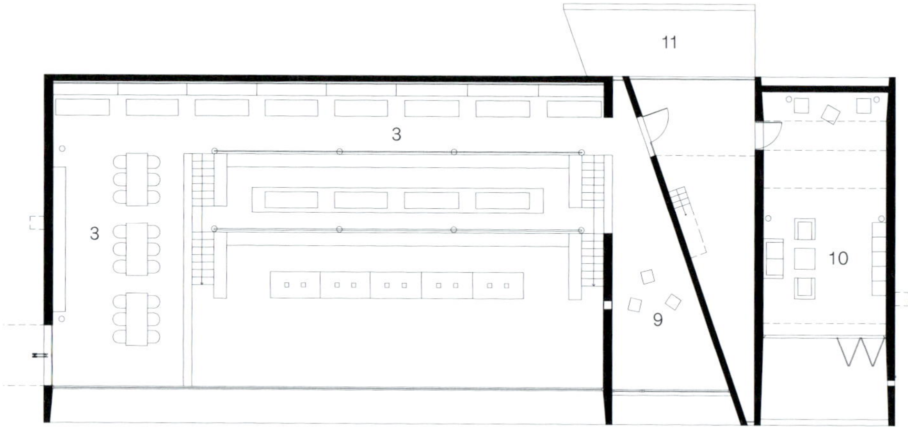

Second floor

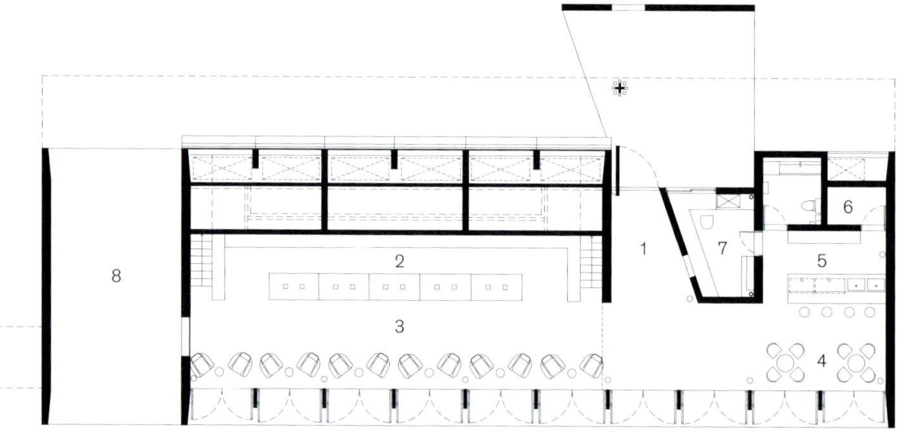

Ground floor

Above: The board-marked exposed concrete animates the interior spaces.
Far left: The concrete and surface quality was tested beforehand using mock-ups.
Left: Mounting the formwork elements assembled on the ground

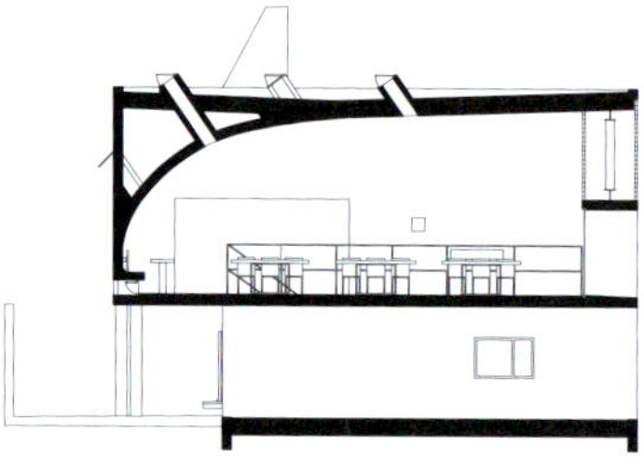

Cross section a

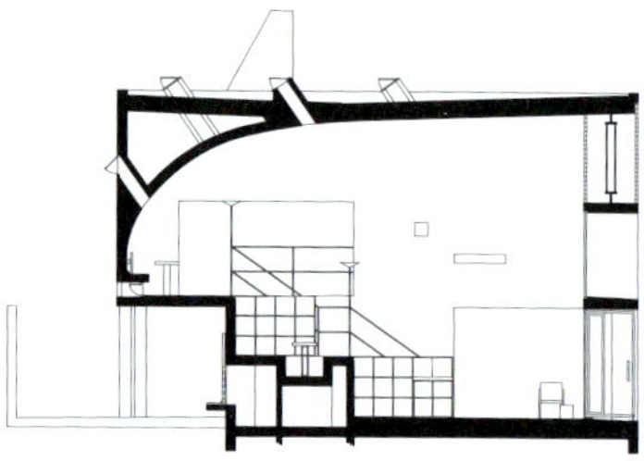

Cross section b

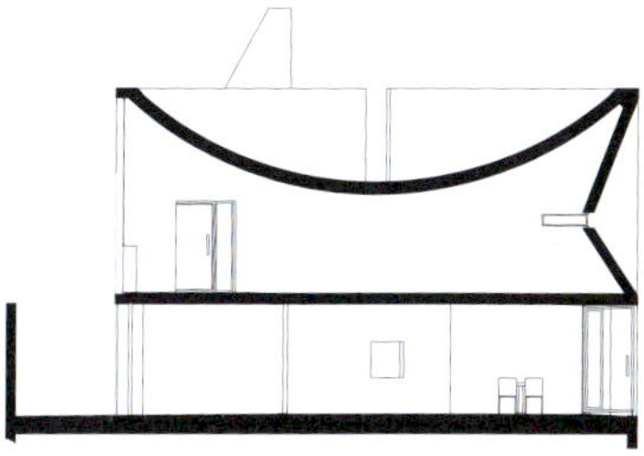

Cross section c

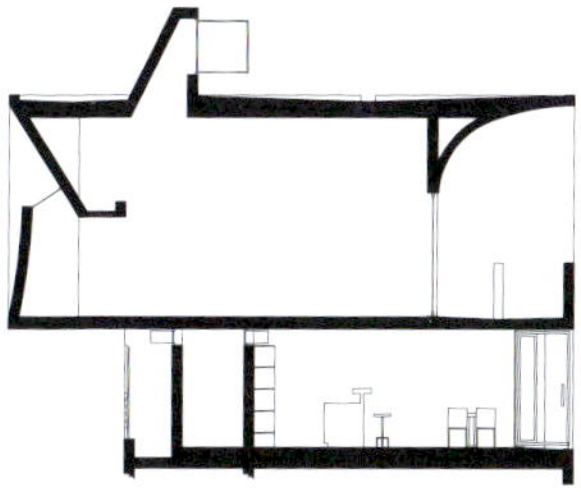

Cross section d

The ascending reading room provides a fantastic view over the ocean.

Residence in an Exposed Location

There is a Chinese TV show on which potential clients for renovation projects are brought together with renowned architects. This is how a ship's captain who owns a small fishing fleet came into contact with Gong Dong from Vector Architects. The captain's house is spectacularly located on the narrow Huangqi Peninsula to the north of the provincial capital, Fuzhou. It was exposed to storms and seawater for more than twenty-five years and urgently required renovation, which was combined with an extension project. In order to support the roof loads, the existing brick masonry was initially reinforced with a 12-centimeter-thick concrete shell. The newly added floor in the roof serves as guest accommodation and a multifunctional space for a wide range of activities. The two preexisting floors were also reorganized. Side rooms such as the two bathrooms were relocated by the architects to the wall facing the neighboring house to facilitate the view of the open ocean and the lively harbor from the building's gable ends. The architects also reconsidered the position and design of the openings in the building. The new concrete window embrasures project outward and provide protection from rainwater. As a result a transitional space is formed which mediates between interior and exterior. Special fittings made of dark wood complete these areas. The new roof shell made of specially impregnated board-marked reinforced concrete is curved to ensure that rainwater drains off quickly.

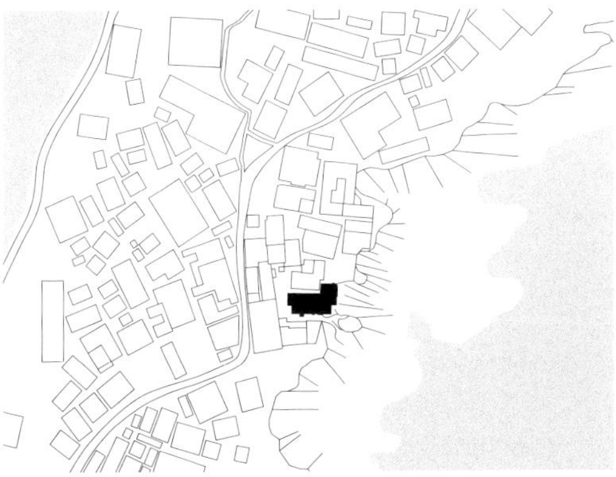

Project name
Renovation of the Captain's House

Client
Private client and Shanghai Dragon Television

Completion
2017

Floor area
470 m²

Construction
Reinforced concrete

The house is spectacularly positioned between the harbor and the open sea. The new shell roof is offset in design terms from the rest of the building.

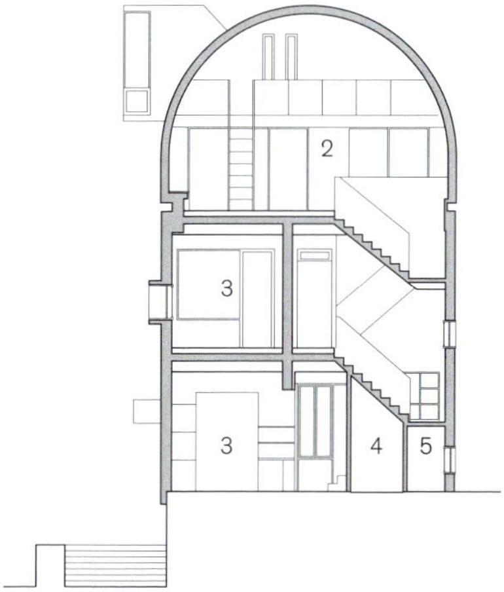

Cross section a

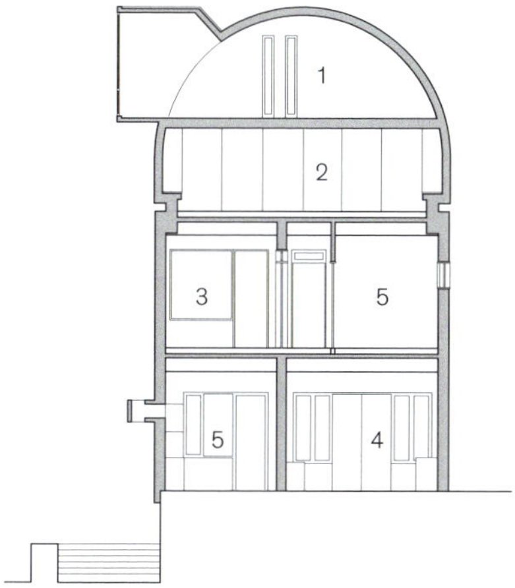

Cross section b

Cross section c

Cross sections a – c
Scale 1:250

1 Mezzanine
2 Multifunctional living room
3 Children's room
4 Study
5 Bathroom
6 Bedroom
7 Entrance lobby

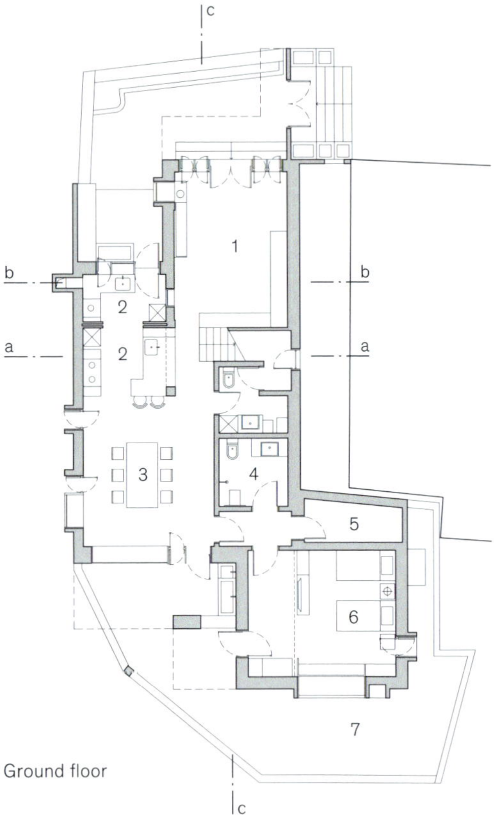

Ground floor

Floor plans
Scale 1:250

1 Entrance lobby
2 Kitchen
3 Dining room
4 Bathroom, barrier-free
5 Storage
6 Bedroom, barrier-free
7 Terrace/balcony
8 Children's room
9 Bedroom
10 Multifunctional living room
11 Water tank

Left: Construction of the new roof-shell using *in situ* concrete
Right: A spacious multifunctional space with fantastic views from both ends was constructed underneath the roof.

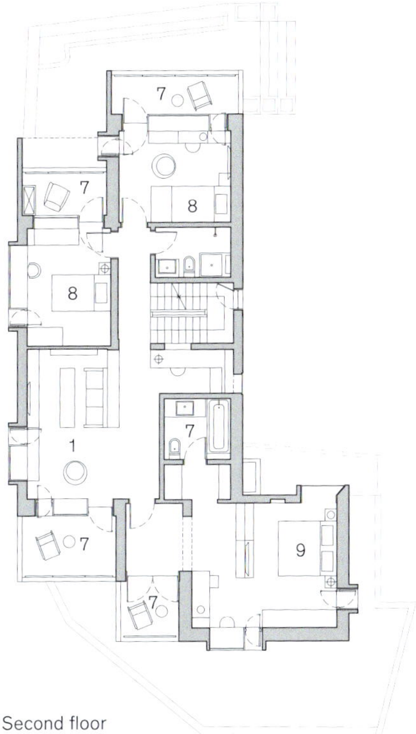

Second floor

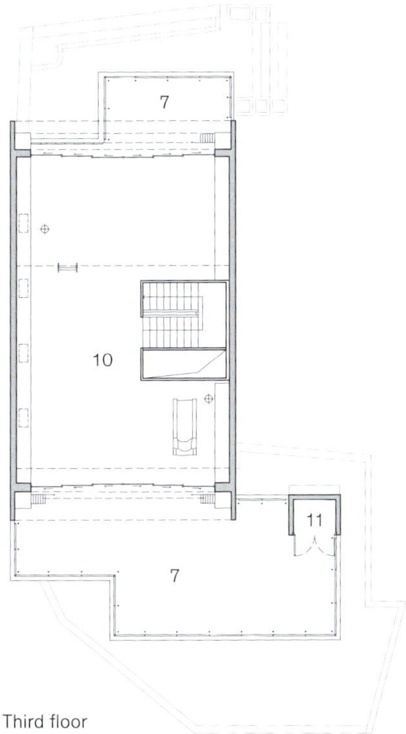

Third floor

The deep window embrasures have been carefully and individually designed as transitional spaces between the interior and exterior. Their wood paneling has been coordinated with the adjacent interior fittings.

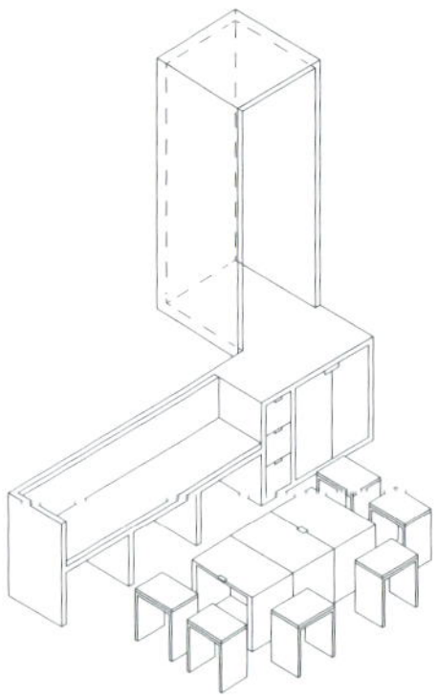

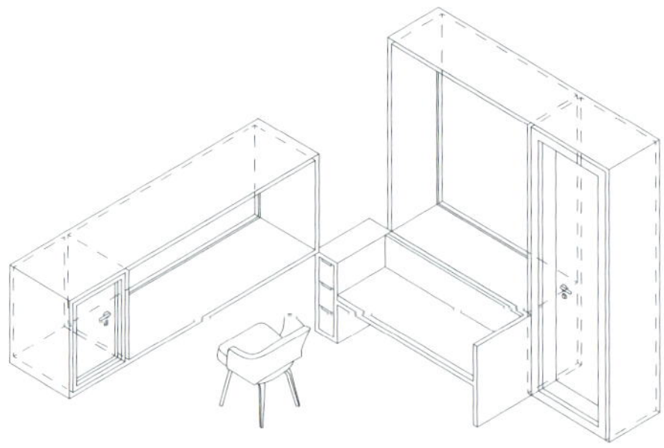

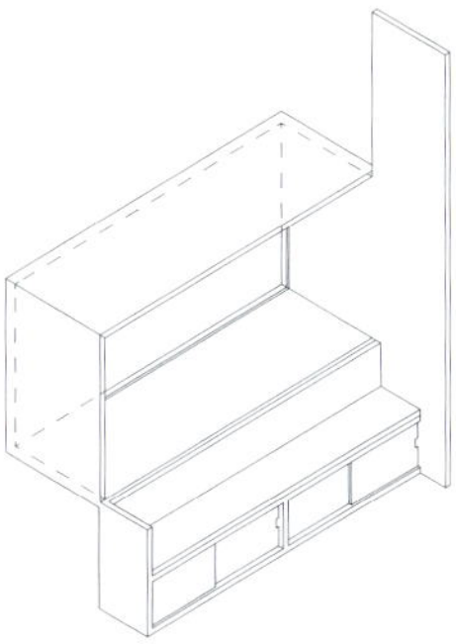

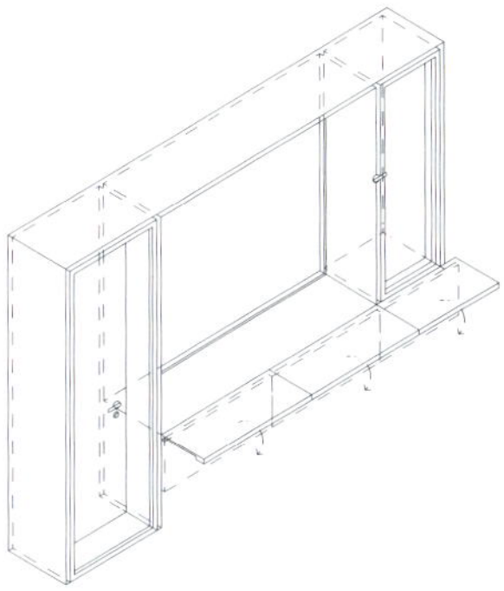

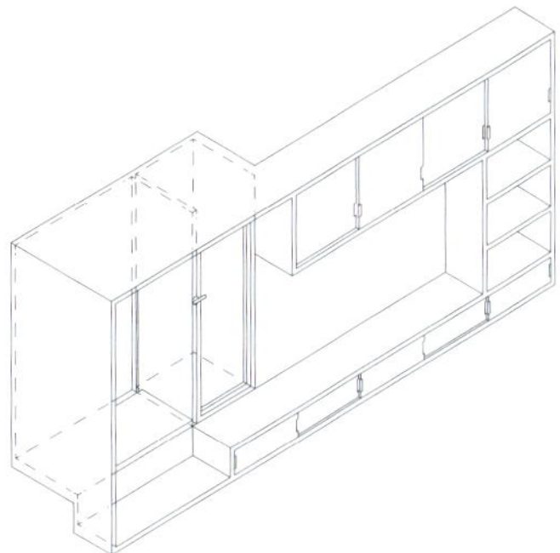

A House for an Artist

Li Bin, who is known for his political portraits, is one of China's most important contemporary artists. His house and studio are situated in an exclusive residential community in Shanghai and have been extended and remodeled several times over the years. The building to the south of the property, oriented to the landscape, had already been renovated by the architect Yu Ting some years before. The current remodeling project now aims to convert it into a purely residential building, while the other building will in future be used exclusively as a studio and private museum. The two structures are connected by a bridge. Above all, the artist wanted a place that was in keeping with his work and could also serve as a source of inspiration. In this context, colors and light play a particular role for him, and for this reason Li Bin himself was involved in the design process. This is evident in the plentiful use of red – the artist's signature color – and in certain individual details. One of them is a red skylight in the outside corner of the living room, which creates different lighting atmospheres depending on the time of day and year. The result is an integrative work in which architect and artist complement each other – very much in the sense of the idea of thesis and antithesis derived by Yu Ting from Chinese philosophy, an opposition that in the end is brought into balance.

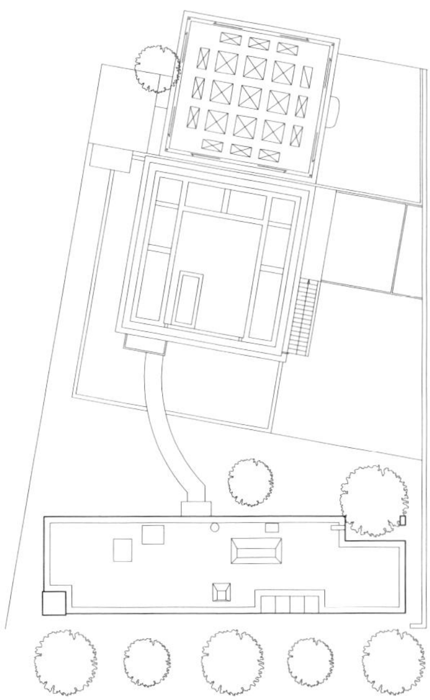

Project name
Plain House

Client
Li Bin

Completion
2017

Floor area
250 m²

Construction
Reinforced concrete, masonry, glass

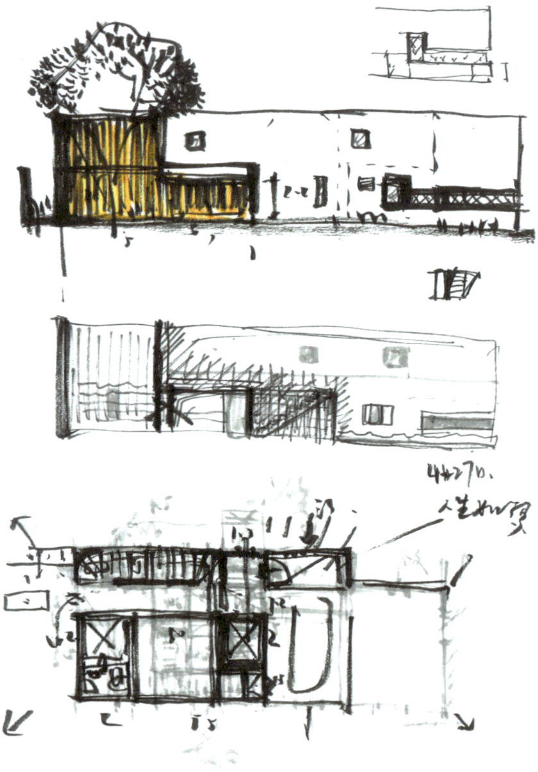

A curved bridge made of weatherproof steel connects the studio building (right) with the artist's house.

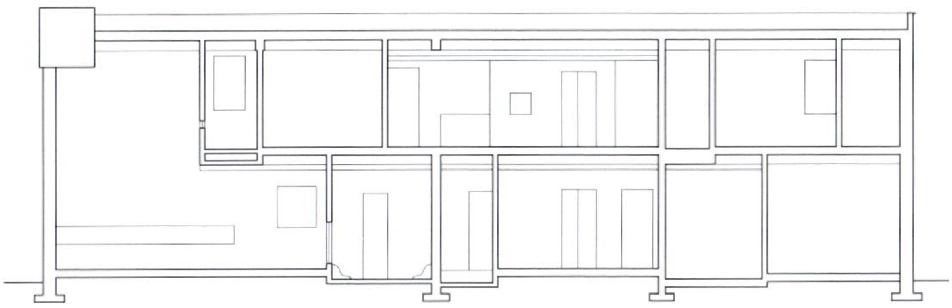

Cross section a

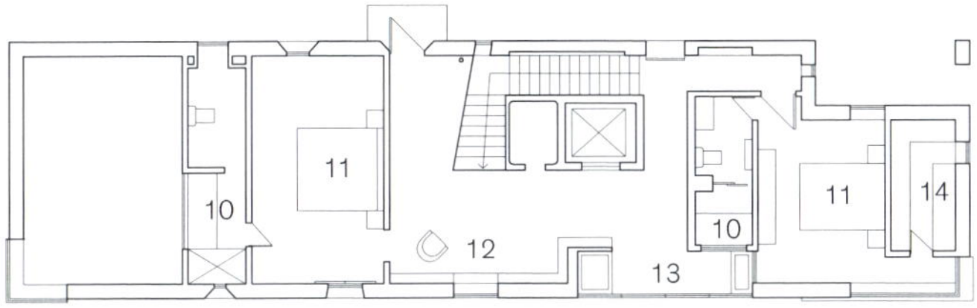

Second floor

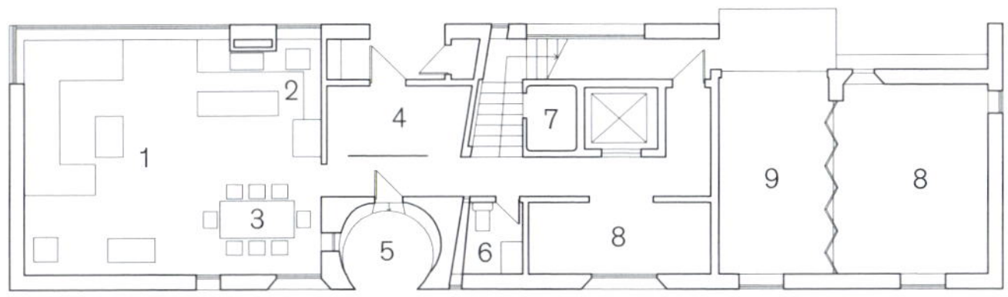

Ground floor

Floor plans, Cross section a Scale 1:250

1 Living room
2 Kitchen
3 Dining room
4 Foyer
5 Tearoom
6 Guest toilet
7 Art space
8 Storage
9 Garage
10 Bathroom
11 Bedroom
12 Library
13 Balcony
14 Walk-in closet

Architect's sketches for the living space extending over two floors

The artist Li Bin in his studio in the north building, which is illuminated by a large skylight

06 Zhang Ke, ZAO/standardarchitecture Beijing

Architecture Office in Beijing

The new studio of ZAO/standardarchitecture is undoubtedly one of the most beautiful architecture offices in Beijing. It is located in the north of the city on the site of a former warehouse, of which only the plastered, closed street facade remains. For the new walls around the courtyard the architects decided to use fired clay bricks typical for northern China. These bricks exhibit slightly varied gray tones, which create a shimmering effect, and quickly develop a sensually rough surface when exposed to the weather. Here and there broken, irregularly edged stones have been inserted between the bricks. The only windows look onto the courtyard: a large showcase-like opening in front of the meeting area and a range of smaller windows that serve above all to provide a view to the outside. Basic lighting is provided by a continuous skylight strip in the roof, which consists of two parts: a flat section on the street side and a slanted section on the courtyard side. The flat roof is supported by a thick concrete slab, which allows for an uninterrupted interior space while also supporting the prefabricated wooden structure forming the slanted section. The firm's founder, Zhang Ke, based his concept for the interior on the "house-in-house" principle. The different functional areas such as reception, toilets, and storerooms constitute discrete units floating in a larger, interconnected space. The surfaces of this space are for the most part made up of a light-gray shimmering lime plaster and a floating screed in the same color. The basic furnishings – elongated work tables interspersed with metal side tables – were also designed by the architect.

Project name
ZAO/standardarchitecture New Office

Client
ZAO/standardarchitecture

Completion
2015

Floor area
1,500 m^2

Construction
Reinforced concrete, brick, steel, wood

The architect's office includes the roadside wing of a former industrial building.
The meeting area features a showcase-like opening looking onto the courtyard.

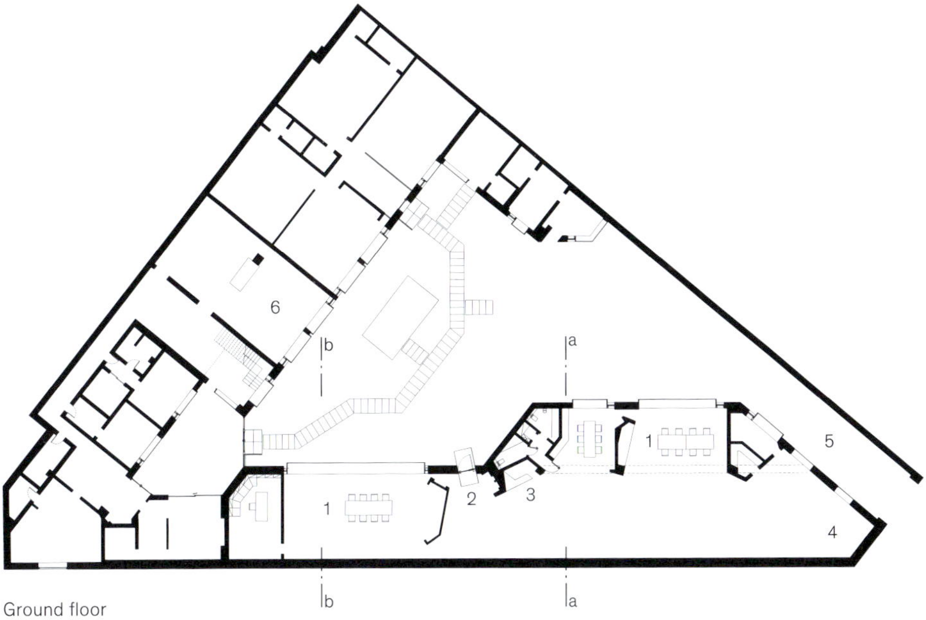

Ground floor

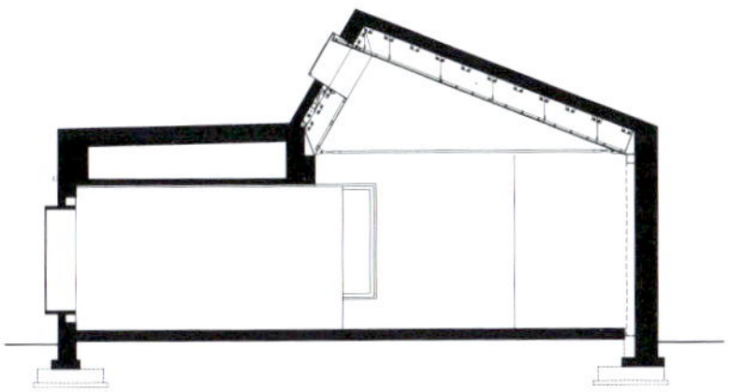

Cross section a

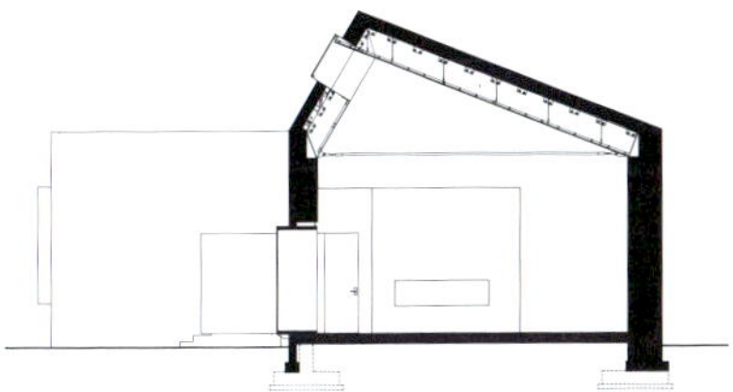

Cross section b

Floor plan
Scale 1:500
Cross sections a, b
Scale 1:250

1 Meeting area
2 Entrance
3 Reception
4 Model-making area
5 Approach
6 Apartment and office of the project developers

07 Zhang Ke, ZAO/ standardarchitecture Beijing

Children's Library in a Hutong

Hutongs are narrow alleys formed by lines of courtyard houses. They are a traditional form of neighborhood in Beijing and were once found all over the city. With his diverse hutong projects, the architect Zhang Ke aims to illustrate the potential of this form of building and to provide examples of how hutongs can be preserved by integrating communal facilities into them rather than, as is so often the case, filling them with shops for tourists and galleries. The 300-year-old Cha'er Hutong – a quiet spot in the lively Dashilar neighborhood in the city center – once housed a temple, which was converted into residences for more than a dozen families in the 1950s. Over the years resident families built small add-on kitchens in the courtyard, most of which were demolished during subsequent renovations. However, Zhang Ke sees in such structures a historical testimony that tells of life in the hutongs during a particular era. Following consultation with the families still living around the courtyard, he installed a children's library made of reinforced concrete and plywood and measuring around 9 square meters under a roof of the former temple. He also redesigned one of the former kitchens into a children's art space made from traditional bluish-gray brick. Standing in the shade of a large ash tree, the tiny building features an external staircase leading to the roof, where children can sit beneath the foliage and look out over the courtyard.

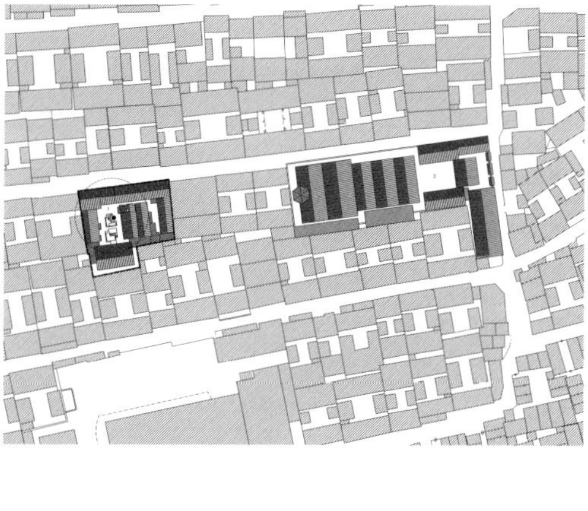

Project name
"Micro Yuan'er" Children's Library and Art Center

Client
Camerich

Completion
2014

Floor area
145 m²

Construction
Reinforced concrete, brick, plywood

The roof of the creative pavilion underneath a large ash tree in the center of the courtyard also provides a play space for the children.

Floor plan
Scale 1:250

1 Library
2 Reading space
3 Creative space
4 Kitchen
5 Dance/multifunctional space
6 Changing room
7 Courtyard
8 Group space
9 Guard room
10 Sanitary facilities
11 Conference room
12 Office

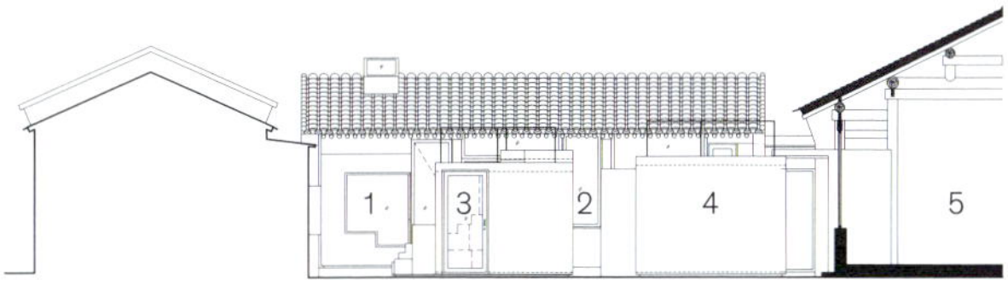

Cross section c

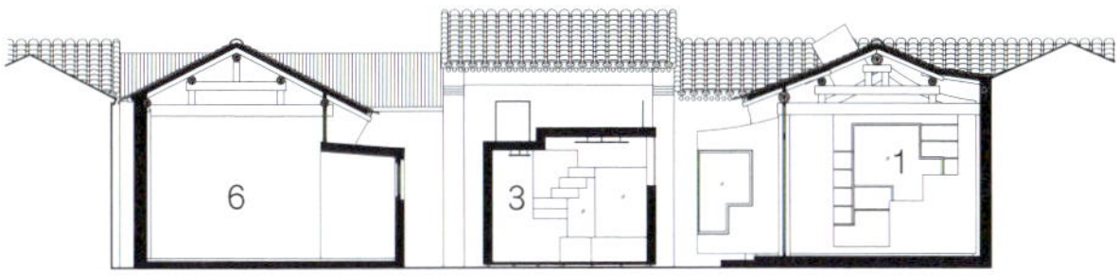

Cross section b

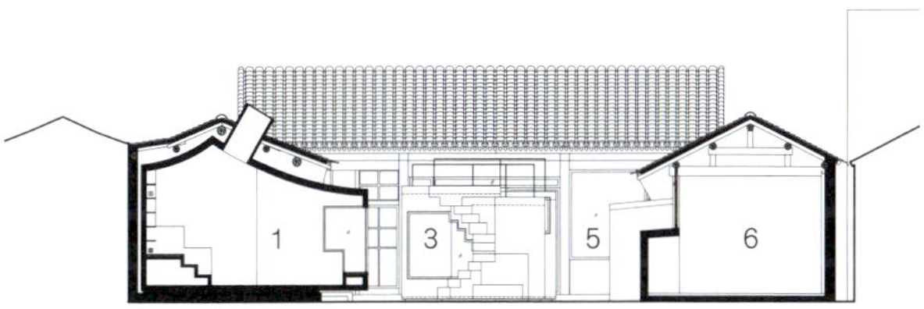

Cross section a

Cross sections a–c
Scale 1:250

1 Library
2 Reading space
3 Creative space
4 Kitchen
5 Dance/multifunctional space
6 Group space

The 9-square-meter library space made of board-marked exposed concrete is located under the roof of a preexisting building made of bricks and wood.

08 Mu Wei, Advanced Architecture Lab(AaL)/ Zhou Chao, Atelier UPA

Sanjia, Guangxi

A Learning and Play Space with its Own History

The village of Sanjia is located on a small river amid the spectacular South China karst landscape. When the village was reconstructed, most of the original buildings were demolished, leaving only a sixty-year-old clay brick building that once served as a private dwelling. Over the years the house was repaired many times before being abandoned and becoming partly dilapidated. On the initiative of a teacher, the old house was reconstructed as a witness to the past and an example of rural vernacular building, and it is now used as a community center and a space where children can come to learn and play. In order to create more interior space, the architects removed the internal walls and integrated a steel structure to support the roof. The clay bricks from the internal walls were then used to repair the outer ones. Skylights were installed to allow in a great deal of natural light. In order to serve the functions planned for the space, the architects also designed a new single-story building structured around three indented courtyards, which provides a strong contrast to the old building. Positioned between the river and the old house, this new building has a supporting structure made of high-strength bamboo fiber composites and walls for the most part made of glass. Clay bricks were only used by the architects in the kitchen, in order to forge a visual connection with the old building.

Project name
The South Yard

Client
Lanchuan Investment

Completion
2016

Floor area
1,500 m²

Construction
Steel, glass, bamboo

The new building with its mainly glazed facade and bright interiors is ideal for playing and learning and provides a meeting point for village residents.

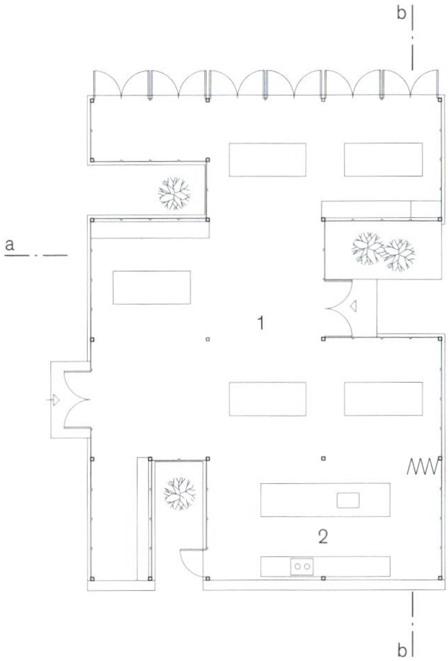

New building

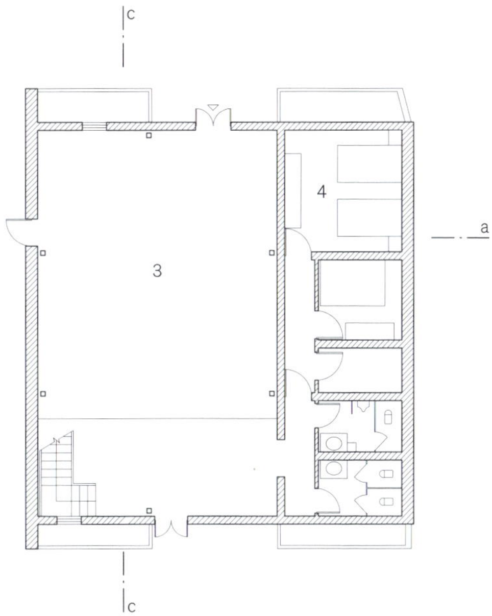

Old building

Floor plan
Scale 1:250

1 Learning and play area
2 Kitchen
3 Multifunctional and meeting space
4 Quiet areas

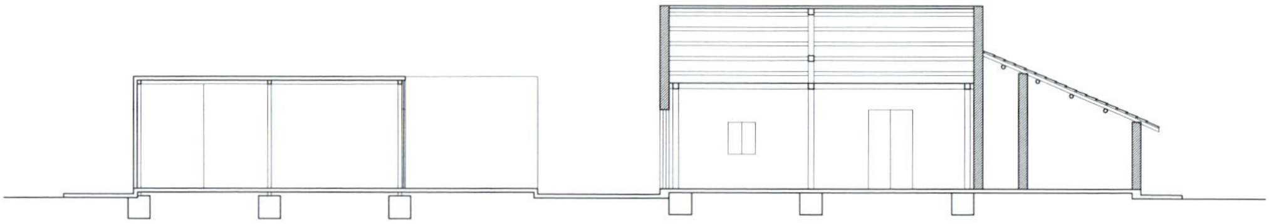

Cross section a

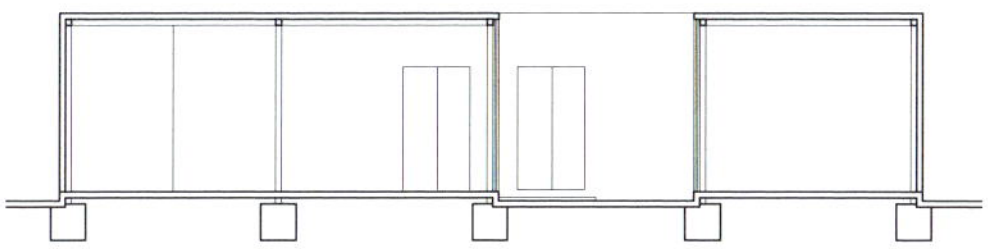

Cross section b

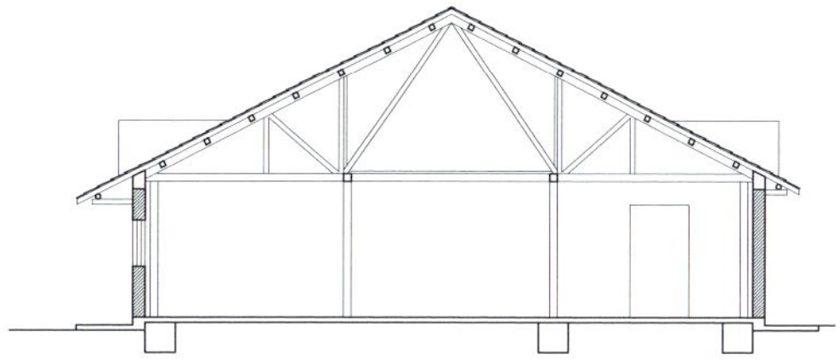

Cross section c

The new building with its mainly glazed facade and bright interiors is ideal for playing and learning and provides a meeting point for village residents.

09 Atelier Deshaus

Xinchang, Tianquan, Sichuan

Kindergarten in the Mountains

The kindergarten is one of ten similar facilities donated by a private aid organization following a devastating earthquake in the Lushan region. It is surrounded by mountains and laid out like a small village, characterized by dimensions that harmonize with the rural environment and the structure of the surrounding settlement. The complex comprises nine individual buildings, which enclose a courtyard on three sides. The architects left the space open only to the west, in the direction of a gap in the nearby mountain range, which allows for a view into the far distance. Local references can be seen in the reddish-gray facades and the locally fired paving bricks. Colored window embrasures and walkways open up the ensemble, which exhibits a clear architectural vernacular.

The result is a structure that stands out from its surroundings while also endeavoring to anchor itself in the natural environment. In terms of both form and spatial organization the design is oriented to the requirements of the children. It often rains in this region, and the individual buildings are therefore connected by a covered walkway, the light steel structure of which contrasts with the warm tone of the bricks. The monopitch corrugated metal roofs echo the surrounding topography, creating a mountain-like silhouette. In combination with the many stairways and ramps, they create an interim zone between the exterior space and the courtyard, which forms a central orientation point as well as a large playground.

Project name
Xinchang Village's Central Kindergarten

Client
One Foundation

Completion
2017

Floor area
1,500 m²

Construction
Brick, reinforced concrete

With its many steps and the covered walkway connecting the buildings, the courtyard provides ideal play areas.

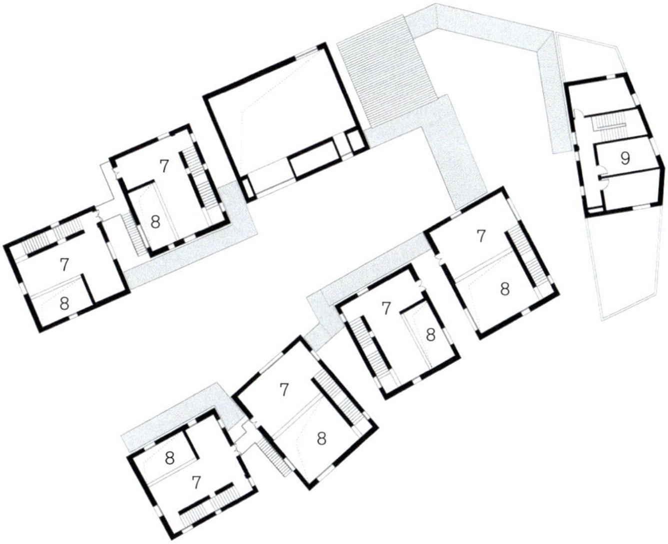

Second floor

Floor plans
Scale 1:500

1 Group room
2 Storage
3 Health care center
4 Security
5 Sanitary facilities
6 Kitchen
7 Sleeping area
8 Open space
9 Office

Ground floor

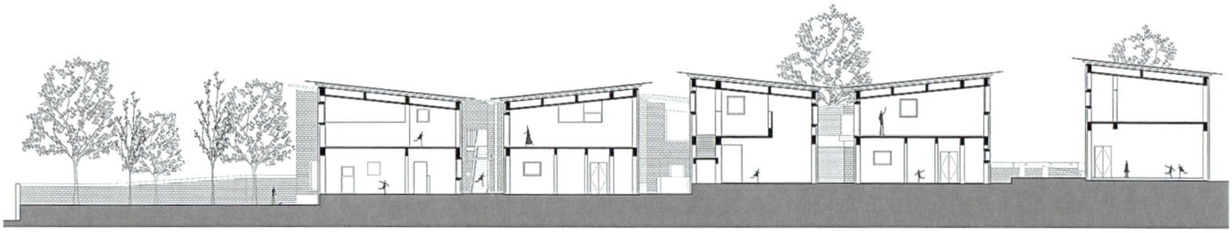

Cross section a

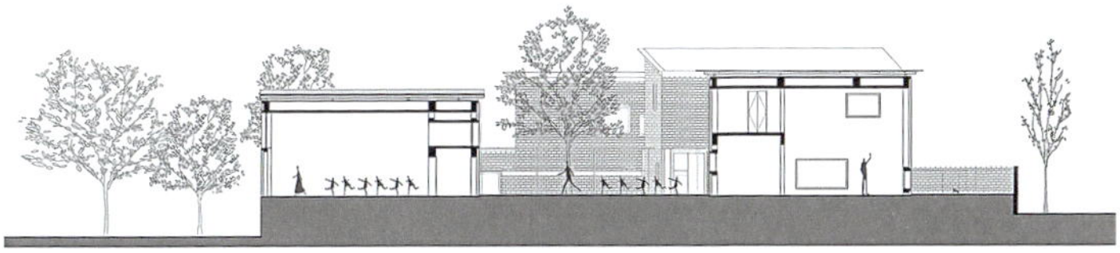

Cross section b

The individual buildings are arranged around an elongated courtyard, which is terraced in accordance with the local terrain and is open in the direction of the mountains.

10

John Lin, Joshua Bolchover, Rural Urban Framework/The University of Hong Kong

Jintai, Nanjiang/Sichuan

Village Reconstruction Following an Earthquake

With this village renewal project, architects John Lin and Joshua Bolchover have provided an example of how reconstruction in a disaster zone can focus on both social cohesion and environmental sustainability. Their not-for-profit architectural practice, which is based at the University of Hong Kong (HKU), aims to improve the housing situation in rural areas. Jintai is located in the mountainous landscape of Sichuan. In 2008 it was one of the places hardest hit by a devastating earthquake; three years later it suffered a landslide. Rather than rebuilding the village in a similar form, the architects, in consultation with local families, decided to erect a very dense and sustainable structure that incorporated urban and rural features. The ground area available for agriculture is limited and so the terraced rooftops have been designed for the cultivation of vegetables. There are four different types of houses, which differ in terms of size, function, and roof design. The staggered arrangement of the buildings produces an exciting interplay between narrow alleyways and expansive open spaces. Strategically positioned indentations in the ground-floor space form entrance areas that promote social interaction. The open ground floor also offers spaces for family-operated workshops and retail outlets, which can serve as additional sources of income. The upper story comprises private living spaces. An atrium provides support for the building's natural ventilation and is utilized for the collection of rainwater. A combination of agriculture and biogas technology based on compost produces a closed loop that contributes to the community's autonomy.

Project name
Jintai Village Reconstruction

Client
Nan Fung Group

Completion
2012

Floor area
4,000 m²

Construction
Reinforced concrete

The new village combines rural features with urban density. The terraced roofs are used for vegetable cultivation.

Site plan

Schematic cross section

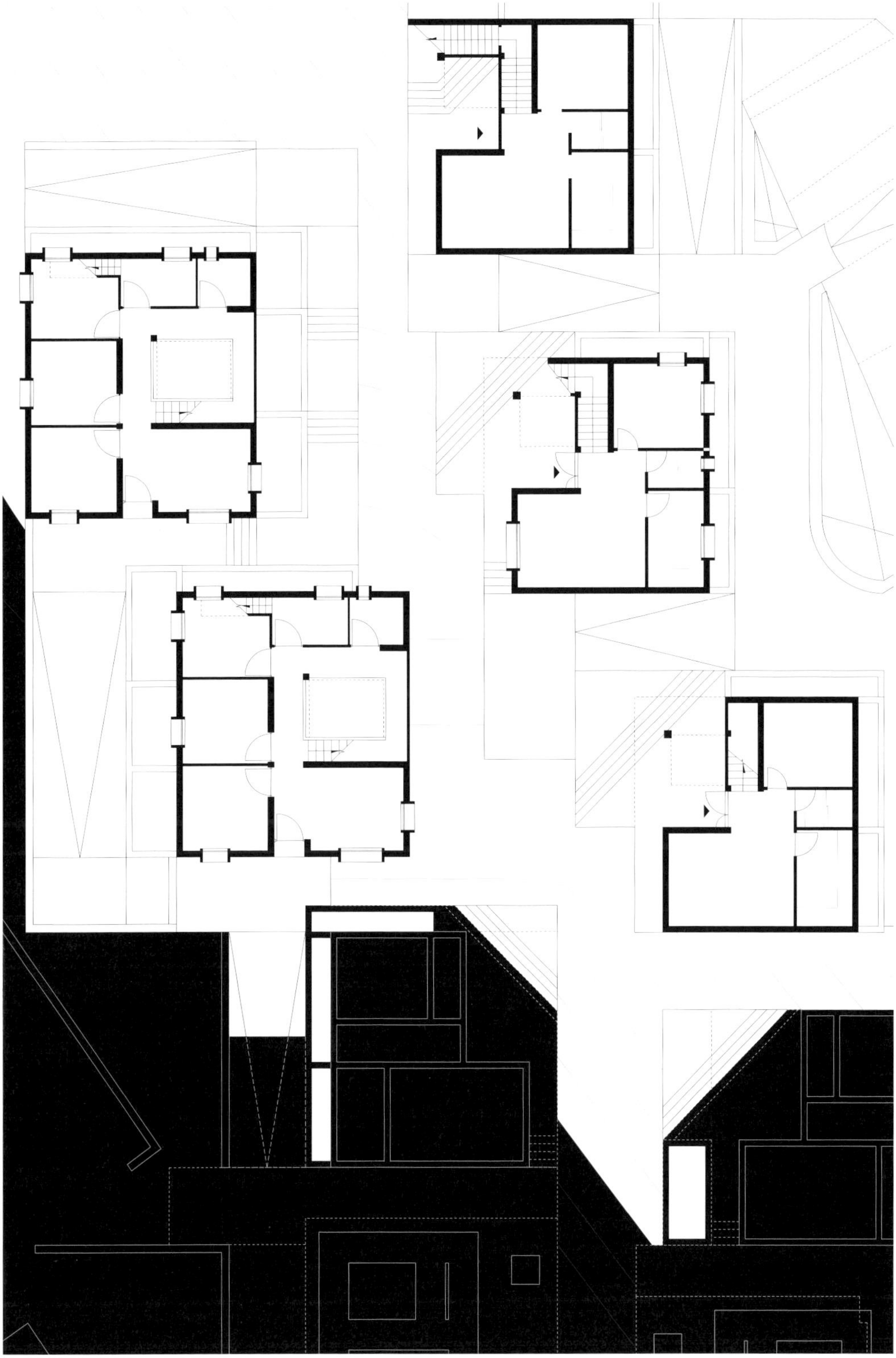

Layout (scale ca. 1:250)

11 Brian Zhang Li, TeamMinus — Yushu, Qinghai

A Visitor Center with a Local Reference

Yushu is located in the far south of the Chinese province of Qinghai. It is an important center for Tibetan Buddhism and the site of the Jianamani, where believers have been adding to piles of stones carved with mantras for around 300 years. With an estimated 250 million stones, the complex is thought to be the largest of its type in the world. A constant stream of pilgrims ensures that almost half the local population earns its living from the production and engraving of "Mani stones." The new visitor center was the first building in the area to be erected following a devastating earthquake in 2010 and has provided the local population with work and new hope. Pilgrims and tourists can find information here about Jianamani as well as public toilets. For the local residents it provides a post office and a small outpatient clinic. The building, which, with its square plan and central courtyard, is modeled on a traditional Tibetan house, is surrounded by eleven connected observation decks, each of which is oriented toward a religious site located in the surroundings. The timber used to construct them came from buildings in the region destroyed by the earthquake. In order to support the preservation of traditional craft techniques, local masons were employed to build the walls made of stones from local quarries. With this building Brian Zhang Li from TeamMinus has created a powerful piece of contemporary architecture that is also anchored in the local context.

Project name
Jianamani Visitor Center

Clients
Office of Jianamani Tourism

Completion
2013

Floor area
1,100 m^2

Construction
Natural stone, timber

Using a combination of rough quarrystone masonry and wood, the architects have translated local building traditions into a contemporary design vocabulary.

Floor plans
Scale 1:750

1 Main entrance
2 Security
3 Passage
4 Post office
5 Public toilets
6 Courtyard
7 Souvenir shop
8 Clinic
9 Stairs to viewing platform
10 Workshop
11 Exhibition
12 Office

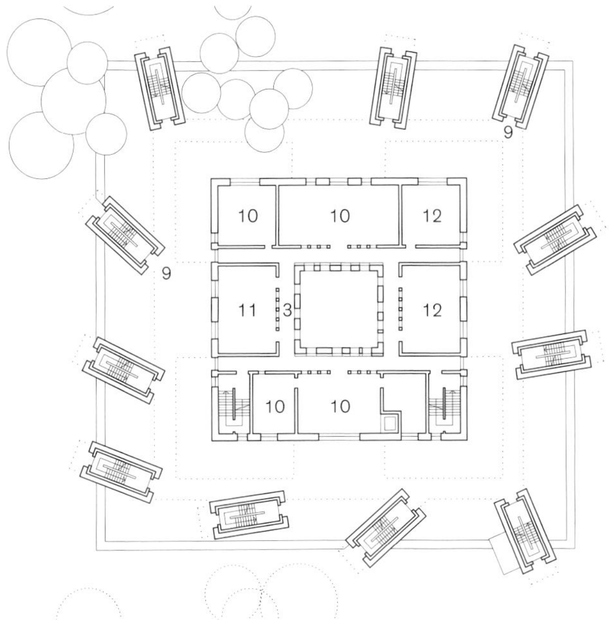

Second floor

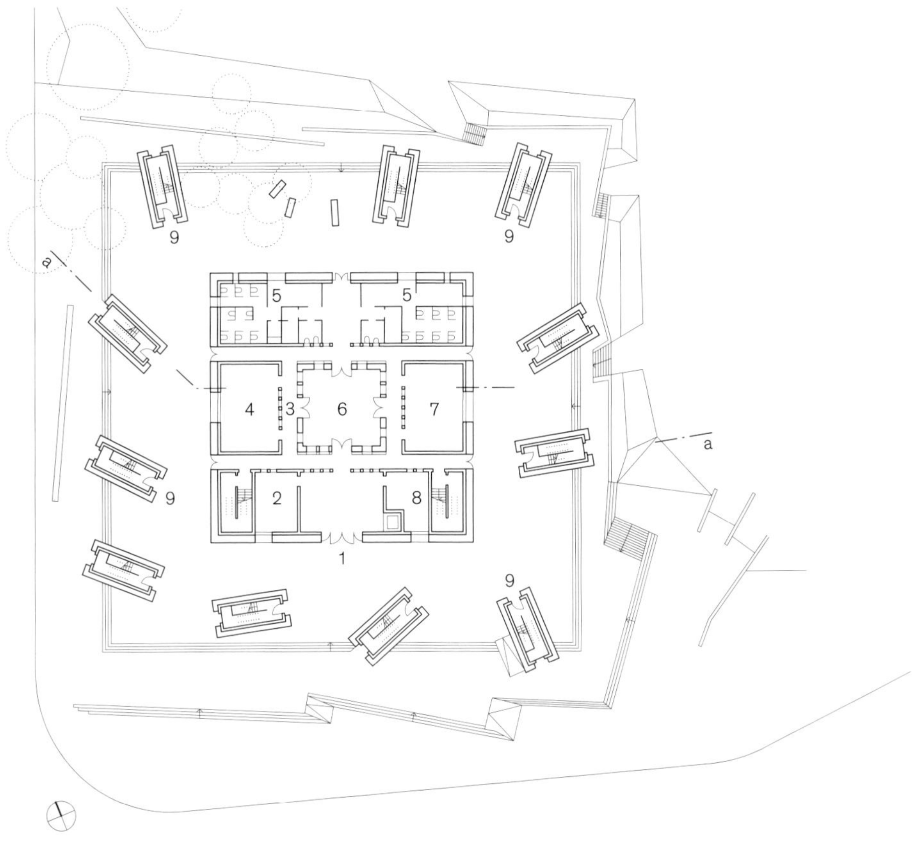

Ground floor

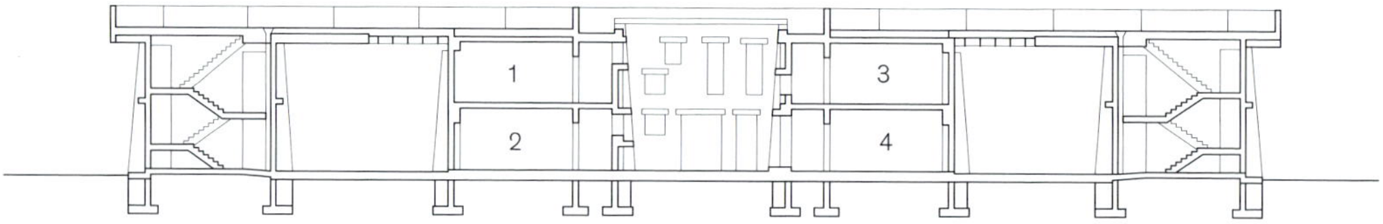

Cross section a

Cross section a
Scale 1:500

1 Exhibition space
2 Post office
3 Office
4 Souvenir shop

In winter a dusting of snow underscores the sensuous qualities of the rough stonework.

12 Xu Tiantian, DnA_Design and Architecture — Xing, Songyang/ Zhejiang

Sugar Factory and Community Building

Like many rural areas in China, the county of Songyang in Zhejiang is being significantly affected by increasing migration to cities. In order to counter this trend, the local government is endeavoring to strengthen the identity of individual buildings with targeted interventions that include the strategic utilization of high-quality architecture. The newly constructed Brown Sugar Factory in Xing, where the population's main source of income is the cultivation and processing of sugarcane, is part of this strategy. A new community building has been constructed between the village and the fields used for agriculture. It serves as a sugar factory, a performance and event venue, and as a place where people can simply meet. During the harvest season from October to December, local farmers use the ovens in the main room to produce sugar. This facility has improved processing conditions and replaced production in farmers' homes. The result is a higher-quality product and, as a consequence, higher market prices. During the rest of the year, the space provides a venue for theater performances, film screenings, and tea ceremonies. The transparency of the ground floor allows for an unobstructed view not only of the sugar production process but also the surrounding sugarcane fields. The design by Xu Tiantian and her studio, DnA, has produced a building that has improved working conditions for farmers while also promoting sociocultural interaction and providing a tourist attraction.

Project name
Brown Sugar Factory

Client
People's Government of Zhangxi Village, Songyang County

Completion
2016

Floor area
1,230 m^2

Construction
Steel, brick, glass

The sugar factory, which also serves as a community center, features a modern design and is located on the edge of the village, directly adjacent to the sugarcane fields.

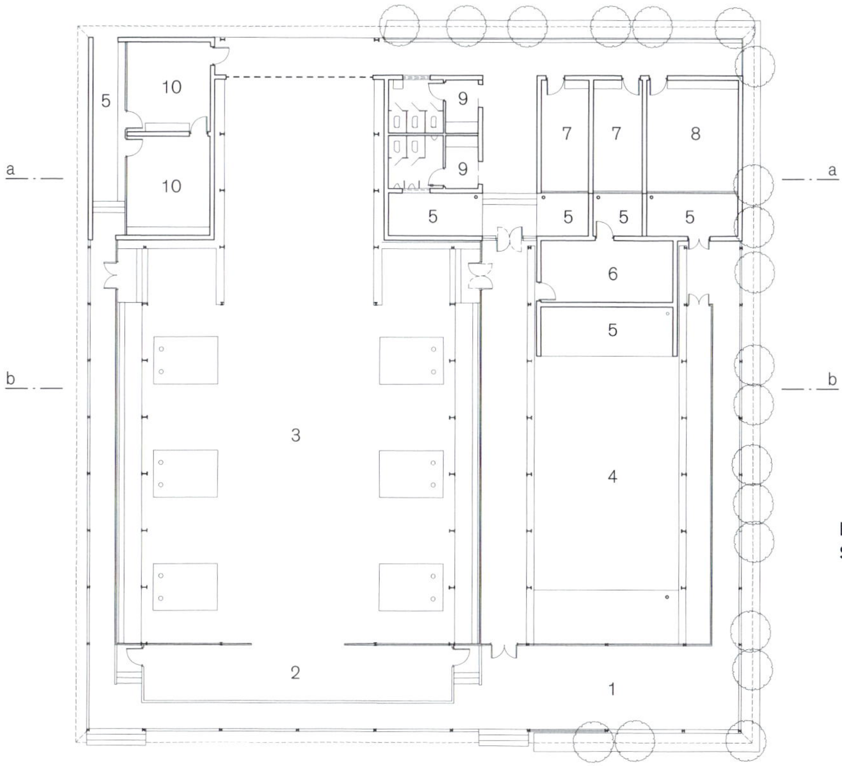

Ground floor

Floor plan
Scale 1:400

1 Corridor
2 Drying
3 Production area
4 Gallery
5 Courtyard
6 Storage
7 Packing
8 Showroom
9 Toilet
10 Office

Above: Large glazed areas afford a view into the production area and onto the sugarcane fields.
Right: The open corridor around the building is covered by a pergola made of bamboo canes.

Cross sections a, b
Scale 1:400

1 Corridor
2 Production area
3 Courtyard
4 Office
5 Toilet
6 Packing
7 Showroom
8 Gallery

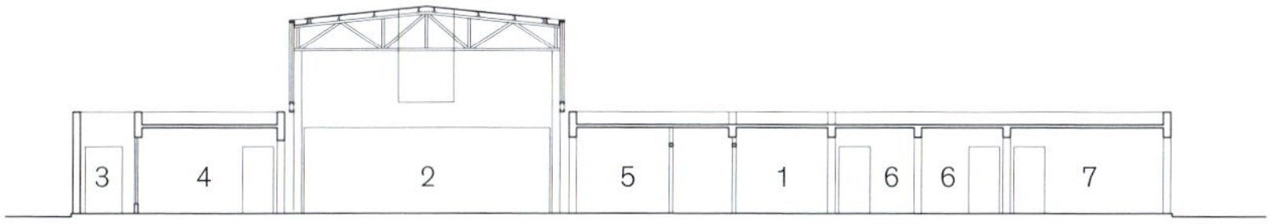

Cross section a

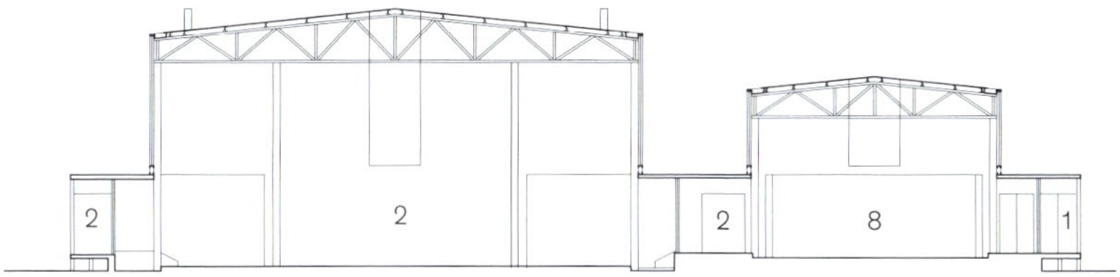

Cross section b

Community Living

With their New Youth Commune residential project, the architects explore new forms of cohabitation by creating staggered spatial zones that include intimate private spaces, semipublic zones, and large, communally used areas. The design was partly inspired by *tongzilou*, a widespread type of collective housing built in China in the 1950s and 1960s. The new complex is located in the northeastern province of Jilin on the edge of the Songhua Lake Resort, which, since opening in 2014, has been regarded as one of China's most attractive skiing areas. Three different groups reside in the building. The two uppermost floors house resort staff, the middle level is occupied by the operators and employees of small shops and restaurants, and the ground floor provides a hostel for visiting young people. The core of all four staggered parts of the structure is formed by an atrium that extends over all levels. It allows light deep into the building, facilitates numerous visual connections, and, running through the different parts of the structure like a busy street, connects the communal spaces with one another. Bridges, stairways, and landings play a particularly important role in the multilayered structure. Integrated tiered seating, benches, and other seating options become lively sites of encounter, thereby promoting exchange and a feeling of commonality.

Project name
New Youth Commune

Client
Vanke Songhua Lake Resort

Completion
2015

Floor area
10,000 m²

Construction
Reinforced concrete

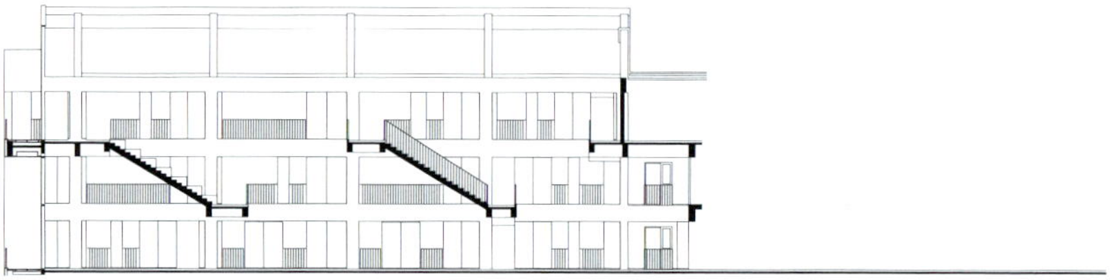

Cross sections a, b
Scale 1:500

Cross section a

Cross section b

Integrated tiered seating and benches make access areas and stairways sites of encounter.

Floor plans
Scale 1:750

1 Private living and sleeping space
2 Semipublic area
3 Atrium

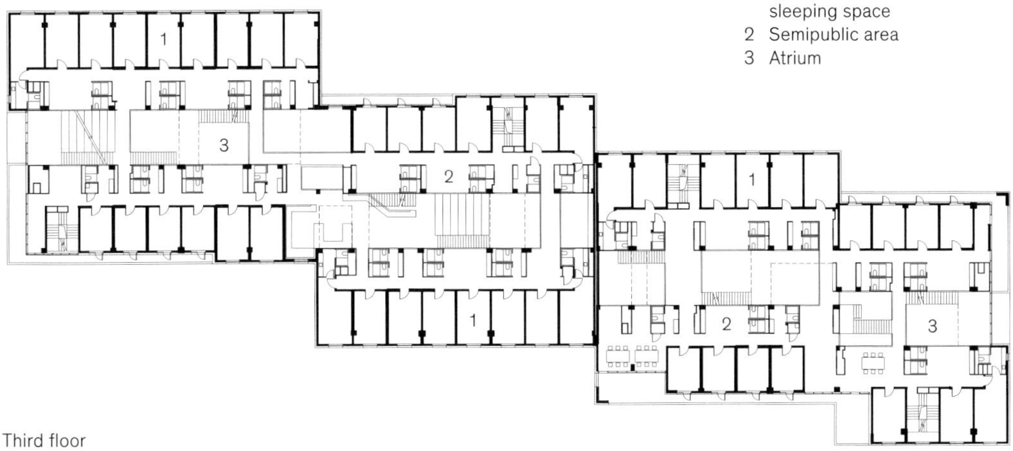

Third floor

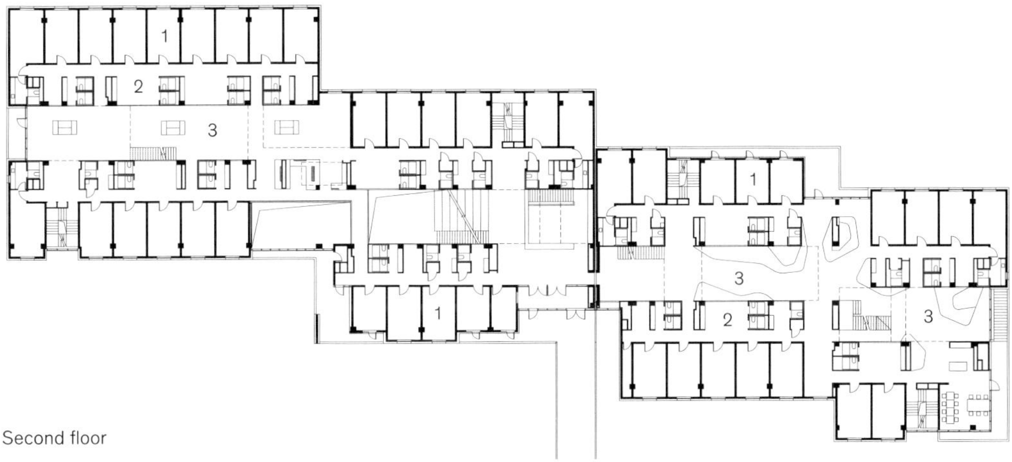

Second floor

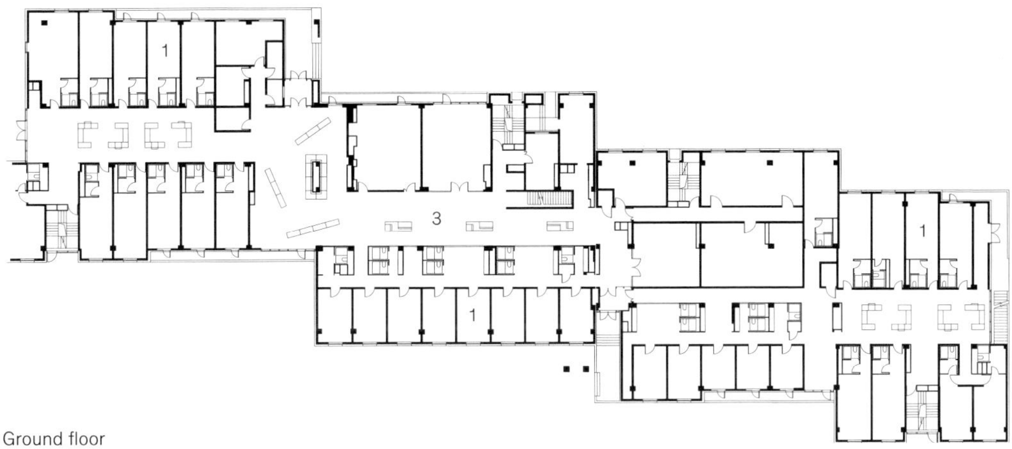

Ground floor

14 **Yung Ho Chang, Atelier FCJZ** **Pudong, Shanghai**

Research Laboratory as Courtyard House

Yung Ho Chang and his studio, Atelier FCJZ, developed the master plan and a research and laboratory building for the Novartis Shanghai Campus. As is the case at the corporation's headquarters in Basel, the other buildings on the campus were each designed by a different well-known architect. A defining feature of the master plan is its application of an urban planning concept based around planted courtyards, which set the tone for the overall spatial structure. Yung Ho Chang also sees his laboratory building as a modern interpretation of the *siheyuan*, a traditional type of Chinese courtyard house. In order to promote on-site interaction between staff members, a semipublic service facility is attached to each of the individual courtyards of the research buildings, and the south side of the laboratory building is accordingly bounded by one of the company canteens. The interior of the laboratory building features a large, well-lit atrium with high spatial quality. In order to facilitate spontaneous encounters between scientists, the individual floors are linked by wood-paneled stairs with landings designed to invite interaction. Additional comfortably furnished communal areas, in which researchers can also work in an informal atmosphere, are arranged facing the garden on each level. Like the spatial concept, the ceramic facade cladding refers to local tradition, featuring varying gray tones that recall the coloring of traditional clay bricks.

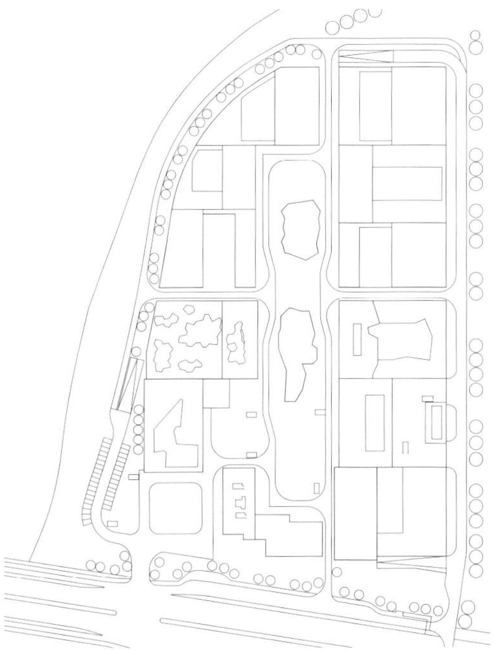

Project name
Master Plan and Laboratory Building, Novartis Shanghai Campus

Client
Atelier FCJZ

Completion
2015

Construction
Reinforced concrete, terracotta

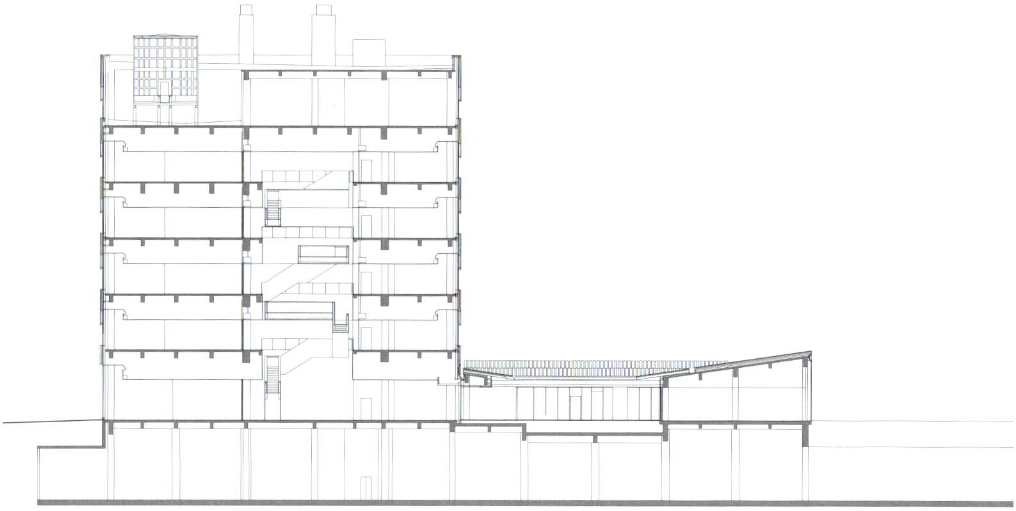

Cross section a

Above: In a modern interpretation of the *siheyuan*, a traditional type of courtyard house, the laboratory building and company restaurant face each other across an open area enclosed on four sides.

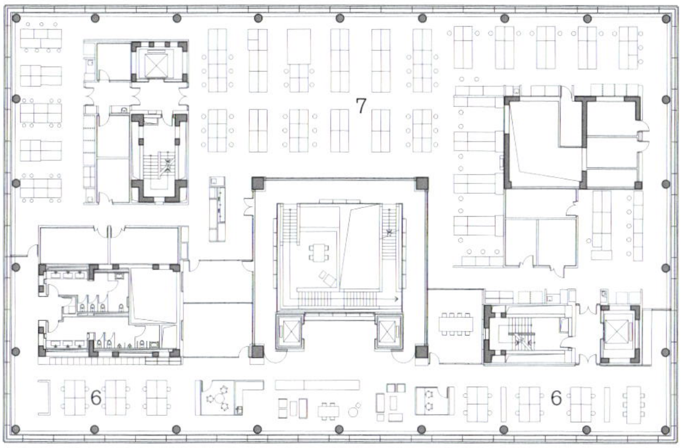

Standard floor layout with laboratory workstations

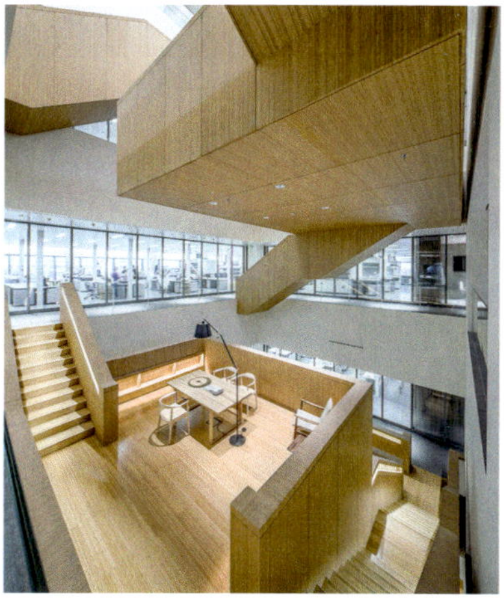

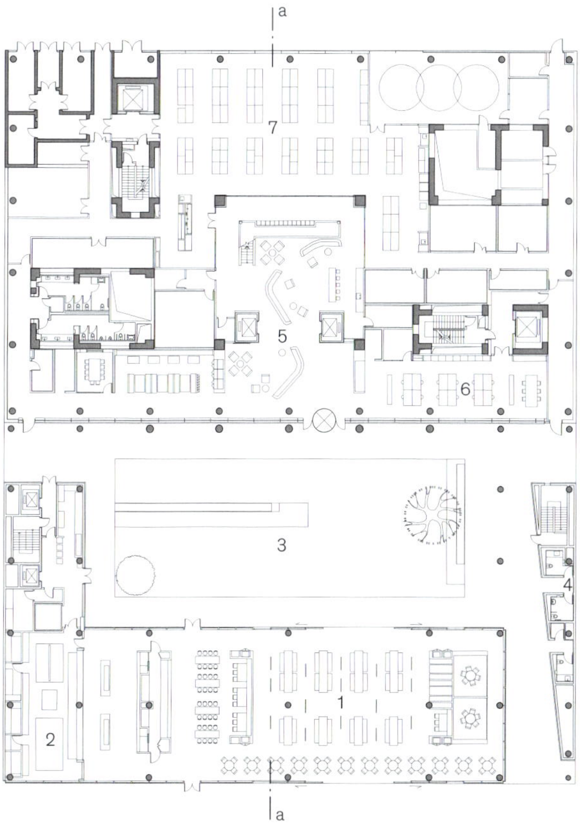

Ground floor

Cross section, floor plans
Scale 1:750

1 Company restaurant
2 Kitchen
3 Landscaped courtyard
4 Toilet
5 Atrium
6 Relaxation area
7 Laboratory workstations

Museum under Water

In Imperial China prospective government officials were selected on the basis of imperial examinations or Keju. In the former capital, Nanjing, a complex was built to hold these exams, in which more than 20,000 examination cells were arranged in straight rows. In the middle of the complex stood the three-story Mingyuan Tower, from where candidates were given instructions. Along with a few other buildings, the tower is the main structure to have survived the demolition of what was once a 30-hectare complex, which remained in use until 1905 and is now a listed national monument. The rest of the enormous area is predominantly occupied by the pseudo-historical buildings of the new "old town." Opened in 2014, the China Imperial Examination Museum guides visitors through the history of this site and the Keju examination system. In order to separate the exhibition spaces from the noise of tourist traffic, Liu Kecheng, one of China's leading museum architects, located them underground. The materials used for the new building, which is laid out along the site's historical axis, hark back to building materials traditionally used in Nanjing but places them in a completely new context. The building is enclosed by three walls. The outer one features typical gray roof tiles, the middle one white plaster, and the inner wall collages made of bamboo. The roof is formed by a large basin filled with water, in which the Mingyuan Tower is reflected.

Project name
China Imperial Examination Museum

Client
Nanjing Confucius Temple Culture Group

Completion
2016

Floor area
27,000 m²

Construction
Brick, bamboo, reinforced concrete

Shielded from the strident surrounding architecture and tourist bustle, the Imperial Examination Museum is located underground beneath a reflecting pool of water.

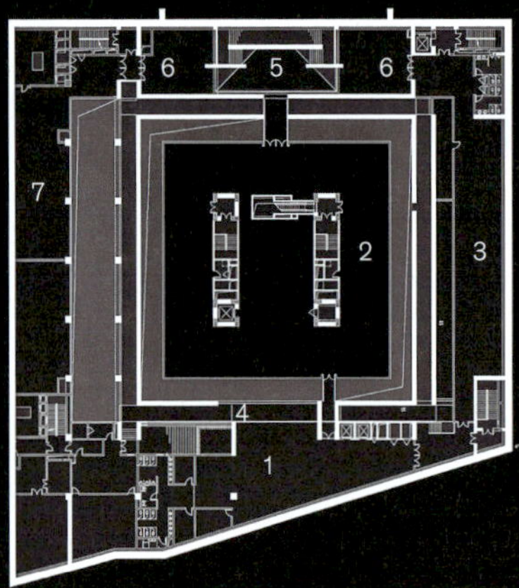

Level -5.10 m

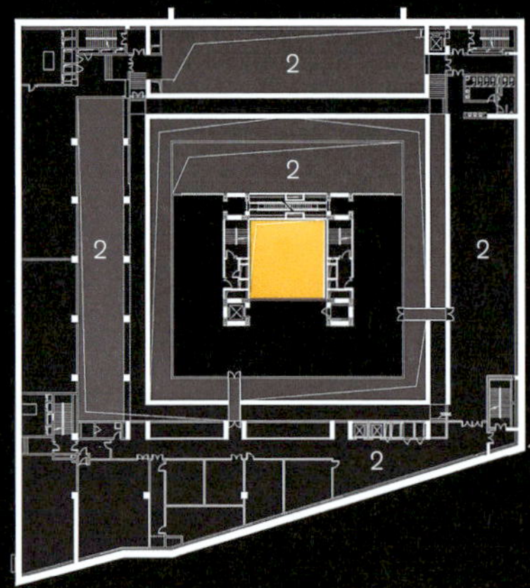

Level -10.20 m

Floor plans

1 Foyer
2 Exhibition space
3 Space for temporary exhibitions
4 Ramp
5 Viewing platform
6 Souvenir shop
7 Shopping arcade

Cross section

Photography Museum as a Seed of Urban Renewal

Lianzhou is located in the northern mountains of Guangdong and has just under 400,000 inhabitants, which by Chinese standards makes it a rather small city. It also hosts the annual Lianzhou International Photo Festival, one of the most important photographic art events in China. The new photography museum is located near the festival buildings and is made up of a remodeled warehouse and a new U-shaped building. The three parts of the new building are covered by a folded roof, which extends onto the outer walls to become the building's facade. The exterior surface is composed of old, layered roof tiles and the interior surface of corrugated, translucent polycarbonate panels, which – illuminated by integrated LED lights – create a pleasant mix of natural and artificial lighting. Openings in the surface have been created using recycled wooden window frames from the old warehouse. An open-air theater has been integrated into the accessible part of the roof, which is connected to the old building by a narrow terrace. The new museum stands out from the buildings around it in terms of both form and materiality while also blending harmoniously into the patchwork structure of its surroundings. The exhibition spaces inside, which vary in terms of volume and form, also make reference to the morphology of the city.

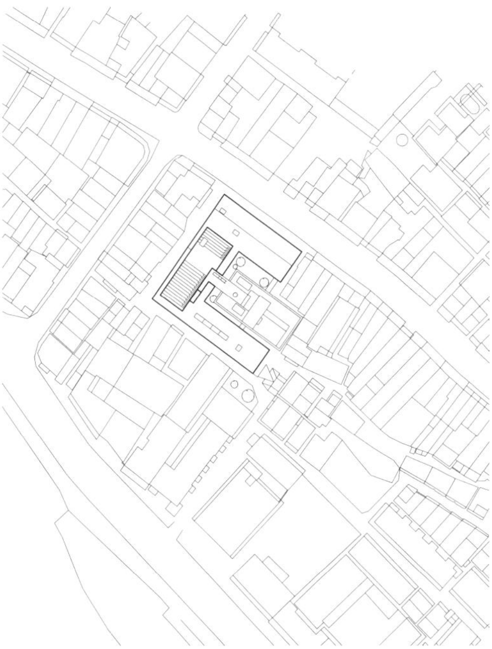

Project name
Lianzhou Museum of Photography

Client
Lianzhou City Government

Completion
2017

Floor area
3,400 m²

Construction
Brick, steel, polycarbonate panels

With its facades made of reused roof tiles and recycled wooden window frames, the new building is integrated harmoniously into the historical structure of its surroundings.

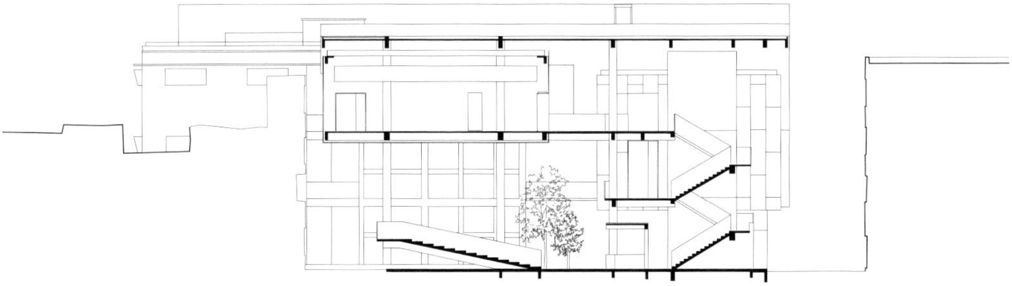

Cross section c

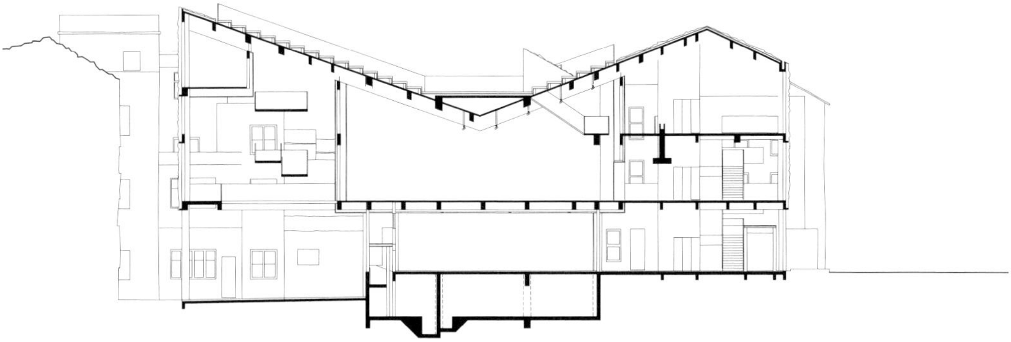

Cross section b

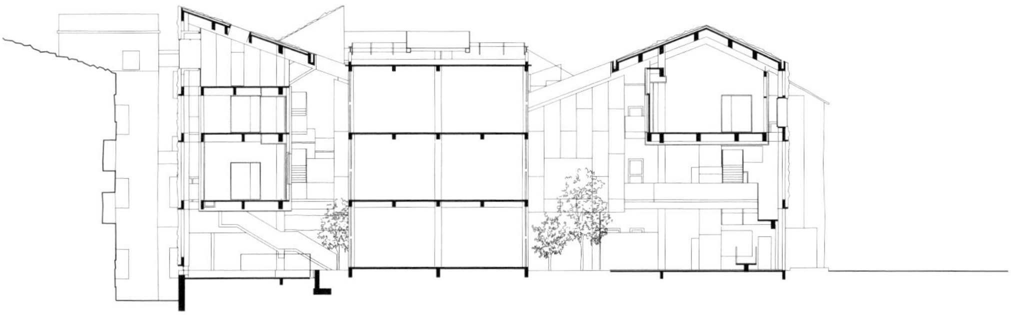

Cross section a

Cross sections a – c
Scale 1:500

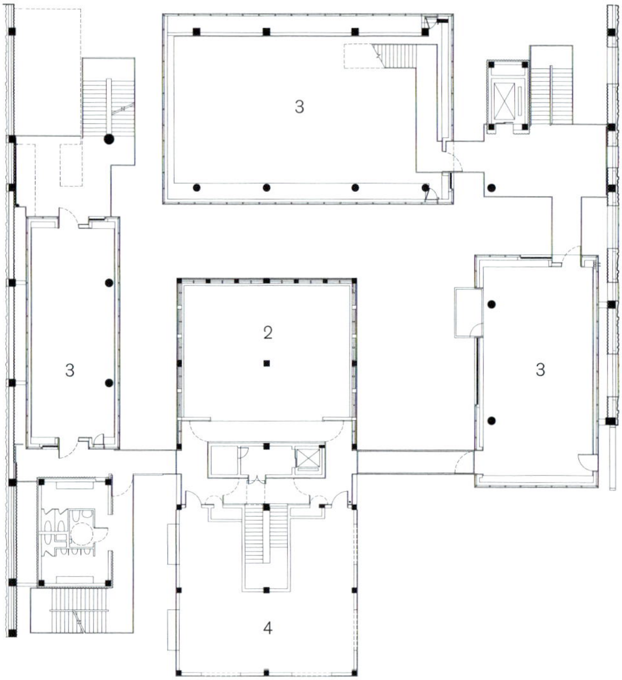

Third floor

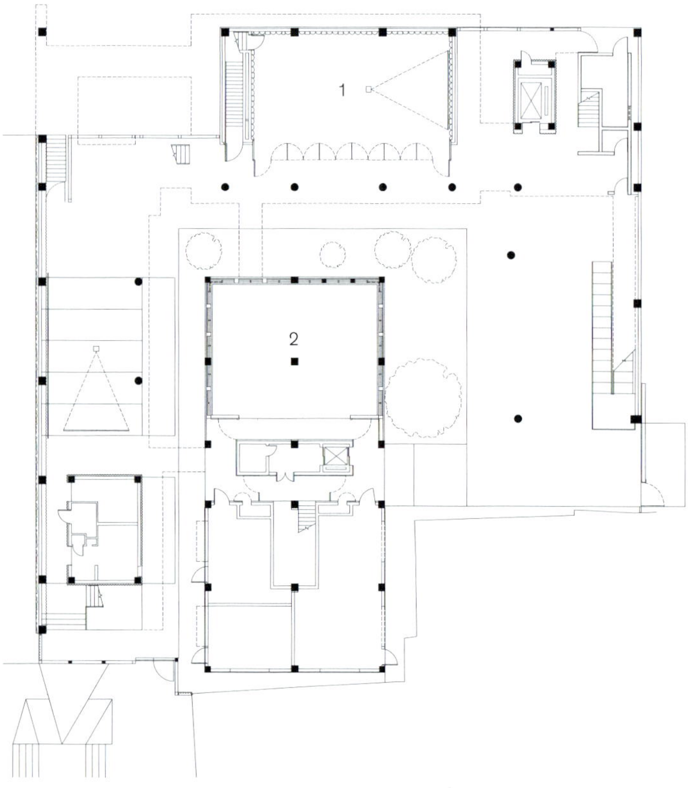

Ground floor

Floor plans
Scale 1:500

1 Lecture room
2 Permanent exhibition
3 Temporary exhibition
4 Storage

Below: Exhibition space and reading room
Bottom: The roof areas of the new building are accessible and can be used as an open-air theater.

UFFLE
LOST

Conversion of a Silo Warehouse into a Cultural Space

Atelier Deshaus has remodeled a number of different industrial installations along the Huangpu River, giving them a new, usually cultural use and thereby saving them from demolition. A particularly striking example is the silo warehouse on Minsheng Wharf in Pudong, which is impressive not only because of its sheer size but also its clear structure, which reflects the rational character of industrial processes. At one point it was the largest facility of its kind in Asia. In 2017, in the first phase of construction, the architects made the ground floor and the top floor, which is 48 meters above the ground, publicly accessible for SUSAS (Shanghai Urban Space Art Season), while also aiming to detract as little as possible from the original design and structure of the 80,000-ton silo complex, which dates back to the 1990s. The most spectacular intervention in the external appearance of the building is a glazed escalator attached to the side facing the river. It links the two exhibition spaces while at the same time constituting a striking symbol of how the former industrial facility has been repositioned. The trip to the top floor affords visitors spectacular views of the Huangpu River and the surrounding wharf facilities, which themselves become a kind of exhibition piece. The artist Zhan Wang clad the lower surface of the escalator in hammered, stainless steel sheets. These provide distorted reflections of the colors of the surroundings, an effect that helps visually disperse the massive volumes of the suspended construction. In the next phase of construction, the plan is to transform the former grain conveyor belt leading from the wharf into the structure's third story into a moving walkway, which will allow visitors to glide slowly upward.

Project name
Renovation of 80,000-ton silo complex on Minsheng Wharf/1st construction phase

Client
Shanghai Eastern Bund Investment Group

Completion
2017

Floor area
16,322 m²

Construction
Reinforced concrete, concrete, glass

Cross sections a, b
Scale 1:1500

1 Foyer
2 Exhibition
3 Silo
4 Ramp to the top floor

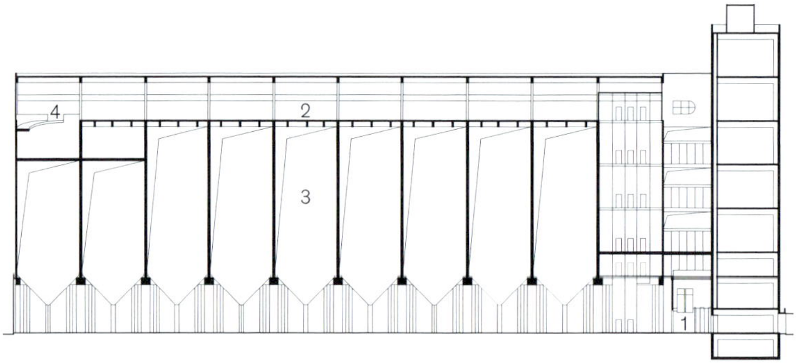

Cross section a

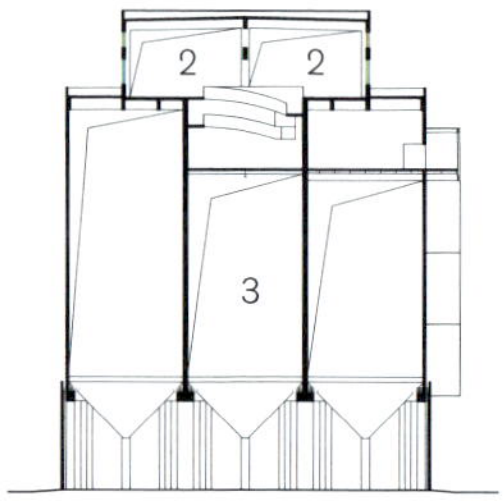

Cross section b

Below: Schematic representation of the basic structural modifications. A new exhibition space has been installed on the roof, a glazed stairway has been suspended from the side of the structure, and the facade on the ground floor has been enclosed.

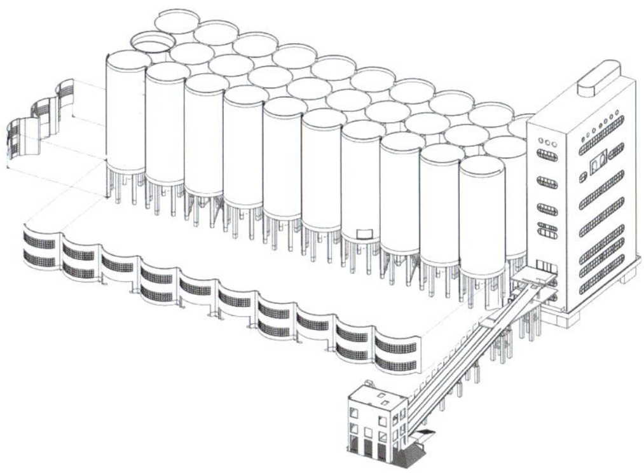

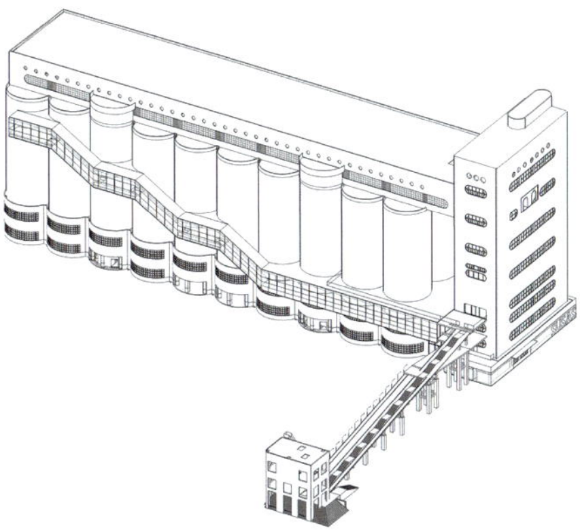

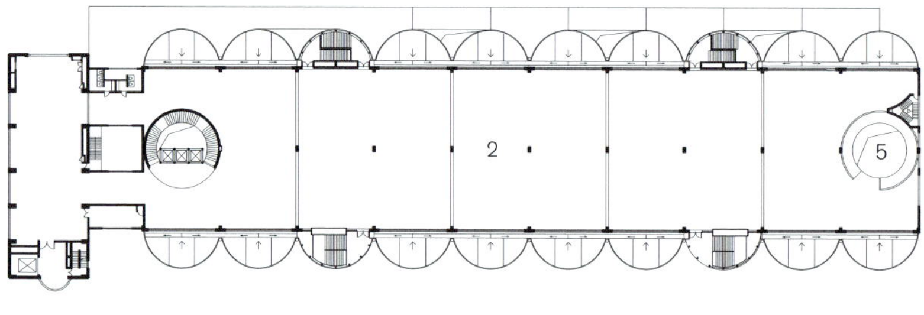

Exhibition space

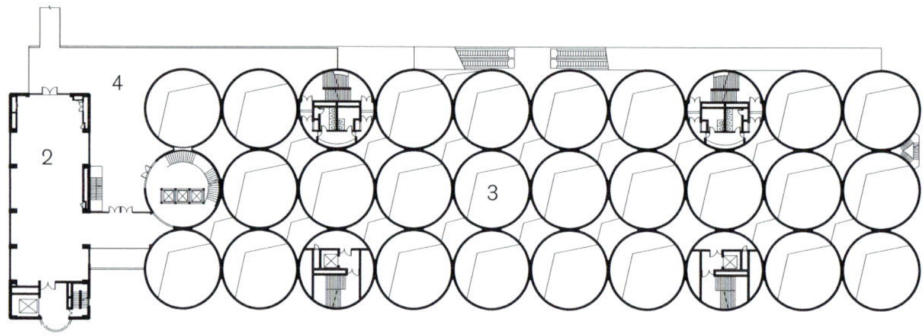

Fourth floor

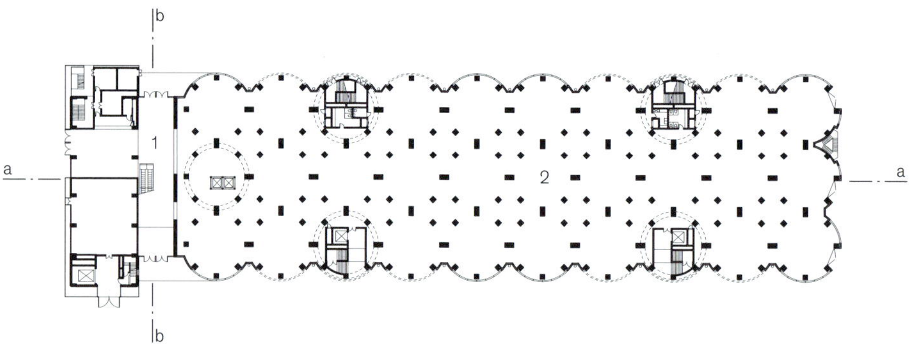

Ground floor

Floor plans
Scale ca. 1:1500

1 Foyer
2 Exhibition
3 Silo
4 External stairway access
5 Ramp to the top floor

Above: Exhibition space on the second floor of the front building

Left: The large exhibition space on the attic floor (left) is accessed via a silo (right).

18 Gong Dong, Vector Architects — Yangshuo Guangxi

Luxury Hotel in a Sugar Factory

Surrounded by steep mountain slopes in the midst of the famous karst landscape along the Li River in southern China, the site of the Alila Yangshuo resort hotel was once occupied by a sugar factory. The lovingly renovated mill buildings from the time of the Cultural Revolution (1969) form the center of the complex and house a restaurant and café, a multipurpose hall, a gallery, and a library, as well as the hotel's reception area. To house the guest rooms and suites, the architects have created three new, simple buildings, which correspond to the original structures in terms of form, materials, and roof pitch. Board-marked concrete and perforated walls made of hollow blocks lend a lightness to the building volumes, whose horizontal alignment contrasts with the verticality of the karst mountains. The longest of the three blocks is divided by three indentations which are intended to evoke the caves found in the surrounding karst mountains and which, with their organic form and bamboo cladding, enter into a dialogue with the surroundings. However, the most impressive part of the complex is undoubtedly the swimming pool embedded in the former loading area extending toward the river, where the old concrete structure of the former crane track is framed by a view of the majestic landscape. The hotel complex is notable for its perfect interplay between old and new elements, and between architecture, interior design, and landscaping, as well as for a quality of workmanship that is unusually high for China.

Project name
Alila Yangshuo Hotel

Interior Designer
Ju Bin, Horizontal Space Design

Client
Landmark Tourism Investment Company

Completion
2017

Floor area
16,000 m²

Construction
Reinforced concrete, hollow concrete blocks, natural stone

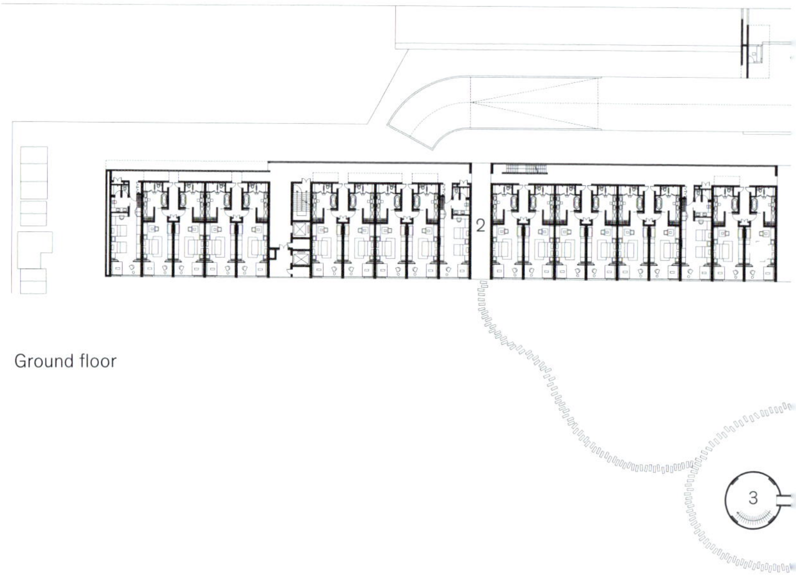

Ground floor

Site plan
Scale 1:1000

1 Approach
2 Main room wing
3 Spa entrance
4 Reception
5 Lobby restaurant
6 Multipurpose space
7 Gallery
8 Library
9 Café/bar
10 Sunken plaza
11 Reflecting pool
12 Townhouse suites
13 Pool villas
14 Fitness area
15 Swimming pool

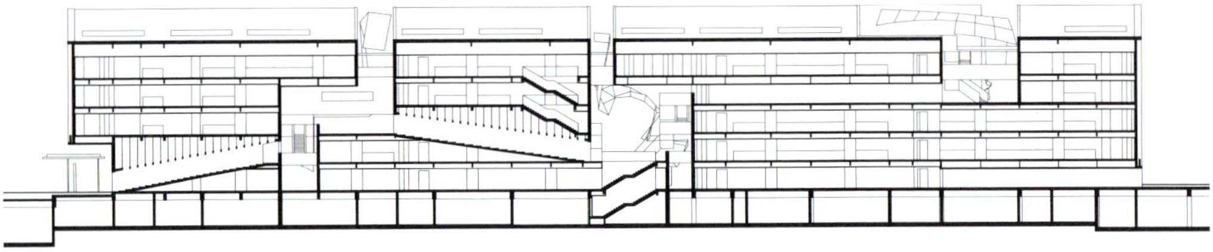

Longitudinal section of rear wing

Northern view of the main building. By night the perforated facades of the new buildings made of hollow concrete blocks and natural stone look like a transluscent veil.

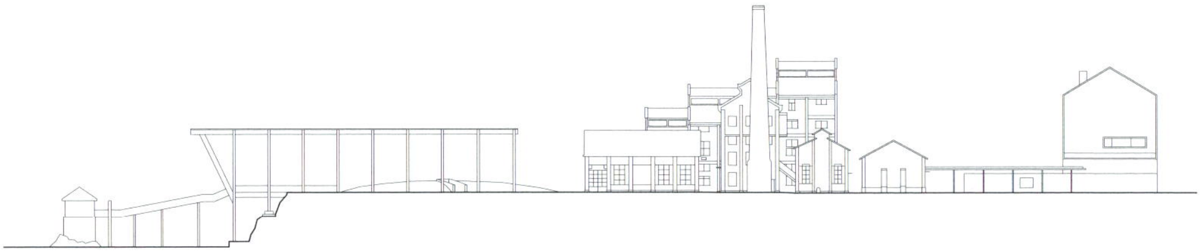

Cross section of complex

The center of the hotel complex is shaped by a landscaped pool of water.
Opposite, bottom left: The surface of the swimming pool on the former loading area seems to merge directly wih the Li River.

Bottom right: Both the buildings and the open areas are notable for their beautifully designed details and high level of workmanship.

19 Hua Li, Trace Architecture Office (TAO) — Weihai, Shandong

A Teahouse with a View

The small teahouse in the Tashan Major Wildlife Habitat in the east of China is notable for the sensitive manner in which it has been integrated into the surrounding landscape and its sensuous materiality, which is typical of many newer projects in the country. The building stands on the scarped edge of a former stone quarry in the midst of a heavily wooded area. A ramp made of weatherproof, rust-brown steel leads to the projecting roof, which is made of the same material and also serves as a viewing platform. From here, visitors can look out over the large Robinia trees and the nearby cliff face. The irregular form of the roof is a result of having to adapt to the position of the surrounding trees. It is supported by six hollow bodies, whose walls feature quarry-stone from the surroundings on the outside and brick on the inside – which is not visible from the tearoom. The two larger spaces house the reception and a bathroom and toilet, while the four smaller ones include the glass sliding doors making up the transparent facades, which provide for an interesting contrast with the solid building sections.

Project name
Rockview Teahouse

Client
Weihai Bureau of Landscape and Forestry

Completion
2015

Floor area
141 m²

Construction
Natural stone, brick, weatherproof steel

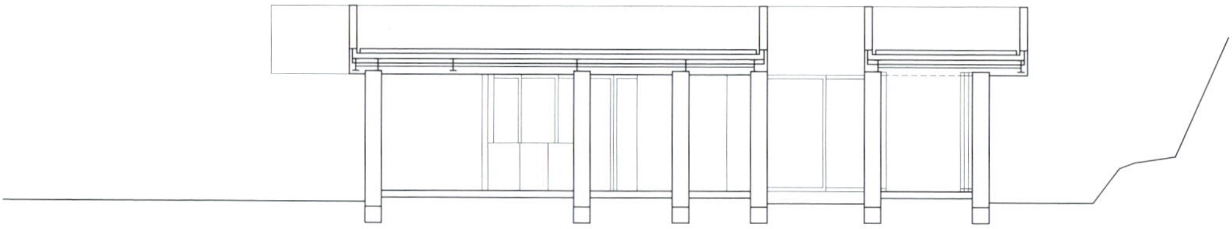

Cross section a

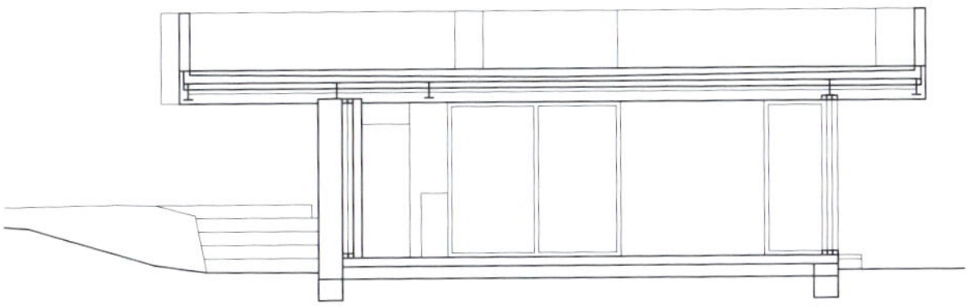

Cross section b

The floor plan and form of the small teahouse with its viewing platform have been adapted to accommodate the surrounding trees.

Floor plan
Scale 1:200

1 Entrance
2 Storage/reception
3 Toilet
4 Teahouse guest room
5 Sliding door niche

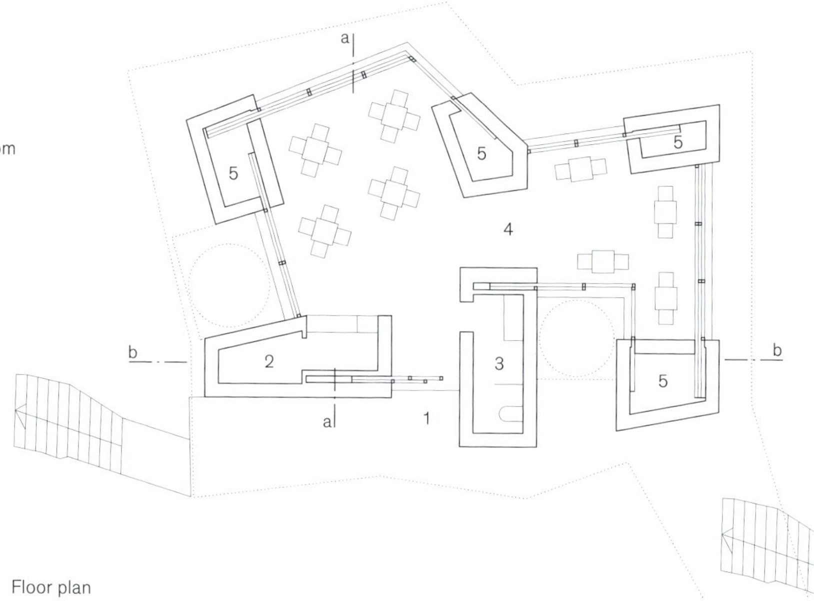

Floor plan

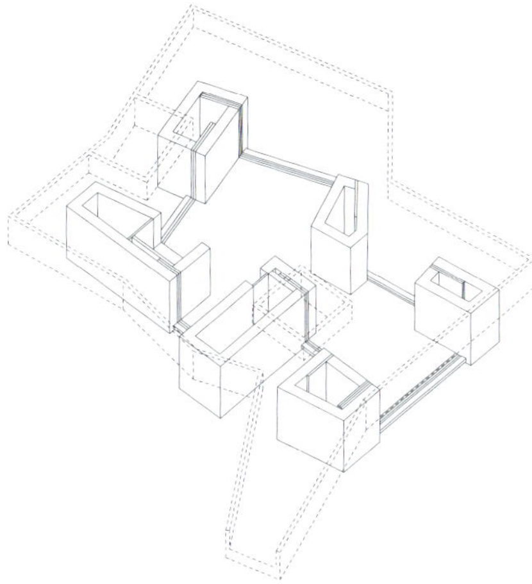

The rough walls made of quarrystone corres-
pond to the viewing platform made of
weather-resistant steel.

Thanks

The author and publisher would like to thank all those who have helped realize this publication, not least Dai Chun and Tong Lingfeng from Shanghai, who provided the impetus for the book, and all the architects and photographers who contributed material to it.

Christian Schittich

Born in 1956; studied architecture at the Technical University of Munich; followed by seven years of work in architectural firms and publishing activities; from 1998 to 2016 editor-in-chief of *DETAIL* magazine; author and editor of numerous specialized books and articles. A regular visitor to China for more than 30 years, he has become fascinated by the recent development of a new and independent architecture there.

Picture credits

All drawings in this work have been produced for this publication or provided from the archives of the architects.

p. 6, 7 Vector Architects/He Bin
p. 8 Arch-exist photography
p. 9, 10 bottom, 11 bottom right, 12 bottom, 13 top, 13 bottom left, 14, 15, 19 top, 20–21, 22, 23, 25, 26, 27 top, 29, 65, 71, 99 left, 122, 126, 127, 133 top, 134 bottom left, 135 bottom right, 135 bottom middle, 135 bottom right Christian Schittich
p. 10 top, 24, 28 Iwan Baan
p. 11 top middle Li Xiaodong
p. 11 bottom left Hufton+Crow
p. 12 top Ziling Wang
p. 13 bottom right Marc Goodwin
p. 16, 59 right, 78–83, 104, 106 bottom left, 106 bottom right Su Shengliang
p. 17, 42, 45 bottom right, 50, 51 left Vector Architects/Xia Zhi
p. 18 Hu Yijie
p. 19 bottom Brian Zhang Li
p. 27 bottom Yueqi Jazzy Li
p. 32–35 Tian Fangfang
p. 36–41 Pedro Pegenaute
p. 43, 45 bottom left, 128, 132–133 Vector Architects/Su Shengliang
p. 44 Vector Architects/Zhang Yifan
p. 45 top, 46–47, 48, 51 right, 53, 54, 55, 129, 130, 134 top, 135 top Vector Architects/Chen Hao
p. 52 Vector Architects/Chen Zhenqiang
p. 56, 58 top, 59 left, 60 bottom, 61 CreatAR Images
p. 58 bottom, 60 top Yu Ting/Wutopia Lab
p. 62, 66, 70 ZAO/standardarchitecture/Wang Ziling
p. 63, 64 ZAO/standardarchitecture
p. 68 top, 68 bottom left, 68 bottom right ZAO/standardarchitecture/Su Shengliang
p. 72–77 Arch-exist photography
p. 84–89 Rural Urban Framework (RUF)
p. 90–92, 94–95 Brian Zhang Li
p. 96, 98, 99–101 Ziling Wang
p. 97 Dan Han
p. 102–103, 105, 106 top Fang Chun, Chen Su
p. 108, 110–111 LYU Hengzhong
p. 112–115 Hengzhong Lv
p. 116, 118, 121 top right, 121 bottom Chaos.Z
p. 120, 121 top left Marco Chen
p. 123–125 Tian Fangfang
p. 136–141 Hua Li

Imprint

Copy editing: Keonaona Peterson
Translation from German into English: Joe O'Donnell
Project management: Alexander Felix, Nora Kempkens
Production: Bettina Chang
Layout, cover design and typesetting: Kai Meyer
Drawings: Ralph Donhauser

Paper: Magno Volume, 150g/m²
Lithography: bildpunkt Druckvorstufen GmbH, Berlin
Printing: Grafisches Centrum Cuno GmbH & Co. KG, Calbe, Germany

Library of Congress Control Number: 2019934235

Bibliographic information published by the German National Library

The German National Library lists this publication in the Deutsche Nationalbibliografie; detailed bibliographic data are available on the Internet at http://dnb.dnb.de.

This work is subject to copyright. All rights are reserved, whether the whole or part of the material is concerned, specifically the rights of translation, reprinting, re-use of illustrations, recitation, broadcasting, reproduction on microfilms or in other ways, and storage in databases. For any kind of use, permission of the copyright owner must be obtained.

ISBN 978-3-0356-1757-3
e-ISBN (PDF) 978-3-0356-1817-4
German Print-ISBN 978-3-0356-1756-6

© 2019 Birkhäuser Verlag GmbH, Basel
P.O. Box 44, 4009 Basel, Switzerland
Part of Walter de Gruyter GmbH, Berlin/Boston

9 8 7 6 5 4 3 2 1
www.birkhauser.com